Usborne Science and Experiments

W9-AFB-089

THE WORLD OF THE
MICROSCOPE

Chris Oxlade and Corinne Stockley

Designed by Stephen Wright

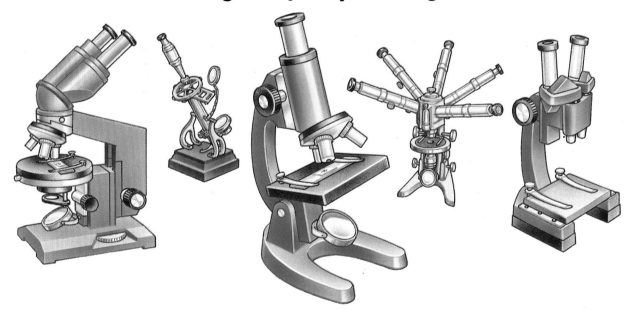

Illustrated by
Kuo Kang Chen, Brin Edwards, Kim Raymond and Joseph McEwan

Scientific advisor: Dr. John Rostron

Contents

3   About this book
4   The history of the microscope
5   The scale of things
6   Magnifying glasses
8   Types of microscope
10   How to use a microscope
12   First microscope projects
14   A first look at cells
16   Simple organisms
18   Fungi
20   Microscopic life in the sea
22   Microscopic life in fresh water
24   Making sections
26   Looking at plants
28   Looking at insects
30   Staining
32   Rocks and minerals
34   Crystals
36   Mounting and measuring
38   Uses of the microscope
42   How the microscope works
44   The electron microscope
46   Equipment
47   Glossary
48   Index

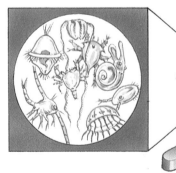

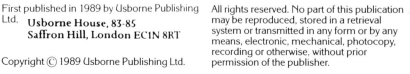

First published in 1989 by Usborne Publishing Ltd. **Usborne House, 83-85 Saffron Hill, London EC1N 8RT**

Copyright © 1989 Usborne Publishing Ltd.

The name Usborne and the device are Trade Marks of Usborne Publishing Ltd.

Printed in Spain   Universal Edition

About this book

Until the microscope was invented, people had no idea of the amazing microscopic detail of the world around them. They were limited by the capabilities of the unaided human eye. Since its invention, though, the microscope has revealed a whole new world, and many important discoveries have been made which have solved important problems and changed the way we think.

This book centres around a basic optical microscope and what you can see with it, but it also shows other types of optical microscope, as well as the electron microscope and the staggering detail this can reveal. All the basic techniques are covered, such as lighting, mounting, sectioning and staining, and there is a wealth of suggestions for things you can look at.

Using the glossary

The glossary on page 47 is a useful reference point. It gives detailed explanations of the more complex terms used in the book, as well as introducing a number of more advanced terms.

Activities and projects

As well as giving you lots of suggestions for things to look at with your microscope and giving you all the basic techniques you need, the book also has a selection of other activities. These all help you to get the best out of your microscope. There are different things to make, such as your own microtome (for slicing sections), and ideas for preparations and tests, such as growing fungi to look at.

Trap for keeping live insects still, so you can look at them.

Applications

The section in the book from page 38 to page 41 covers the different uses of the microscope in the modern world. Ranging from quality control in industry to examining blood smears in hospitals, these may give you some ideas about careers which use microscopy.

This man is using a special microscope to check the quality of a cut diamond.

The history of the microscope

Four hundred years ago, the world of the microscope was unexplored. The structure of the plants and animals we knew was a mystery, and there were thousands more tiny plants and animals we did not even know about. The causes of disease could only be guessed at and medical science was unknown. The invention of the microscope brought about a revolution in scientific knowledge.

It has been known for over 2000 years that glass bends light, but the first accurate lenses were not made until about the year 1300. Around the year 1600, it was discovered that optical instruments could be made by combining lenses.

Elaborate 1755 microscope

The word microscope comes from the words micro, meaning very small, and scope, meaning an instrument for looking at objects. Anything which is too small for the eye to see is known as microscopic.

Antonie van Leeuwenhoek was a Dutch scientist and one of the pioneers of microscopy in the late 17th century. He made his own simple microscopes which had a single lens and were hand-held. He made many drawings of what he saw and discovered bacteria, although he did not know what they were.

One of van Leeuwenhoek's microscopes

In the mid 17th century, Robert Hooke drew pictures of cork seen through his microscope. Like van Leeuwenhoek, he did not know exactly what he had seen.

Hooke drew pictures of cork cells.

Hooke's microscope

All the early microscopists saw very distorted images due to the low quality of the glass and imperfect shape of their lenses. Lenses improved a lot through the 19th century, and the microscope as we know it was gradually developed.

Make a simple microscope

Here you can find out how to make a model of van Leeuwenhoek's single-lens microscope. It uses a water droplet instead of glass. It will show you how difficult life was for early microscopists.

Cut a piece of stiff card 10cm by 3cm and make a hole at one end with a hole punch, or with a drawing pin and a sharp pencil.

3cm

10cm

Hole should be about 5mm wide.

Piece of stiff card

Put a small piece of clear plastic (possibly from food packaging) over the hole, and stick it down with sticky tape.

Tape   Plastic

Dip a pencil into some water and hold it above the plastic over the hole. Try to get a drop of water to fall over the hole.

Drop water over hole

Hold the microscope very close to your eye and look through the drop. Move very close to the object you want to look at. It should appear greatly magnified.

Newspaper print is a good thing to start with.

Water-drop lens above hole

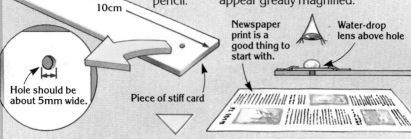

Your image will not be very bright or very clear, but it is probably as good as the ones seen by early microscopists. If it is very distorted, your water drop is probably not round, so try again.

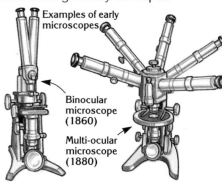

Examples of early microscopes

Binocular microscope (1860)

Multi-ocular microscope (1880)

In 1933, the first electron microscope was built. This type of microscope can magnify things hundreds of times more than optical microscopes (see pages 44-45).

The scale of things

Instruments like the microscope and telescope have led us to discover many things which were too small or too far away to see before. We have been able to place ourselves within the scale of sizes in the universe.

Very large, or very small numbers have lots of zeros in them. To save writing all these, the numbers are often written in a special way. For example, 1 000 (one thousand) is written 10^3 and 1 000 000 (one million) is written 10^6. Numbers less than one have a negative number above the ten, so 0.001 is written 10^{-3} and 0.000 001 is written 10^{-6}. The number written above the ten is the same as the number of zeros.

The distance to the sun is over 10^{11} metres — the actual distance is 150 million kilometres. In inner space and on earth, distances are usually measured in kilometres (one kilometre equals 1 000 metres).

The distance light travels in a year. It is called a light year and is used to describe distances in outer space. It is 10 000 light years across our galaxy.

The tallest buildings are about 500 metres high.

The distance to the moon is over 10^8 metres — the actual distance is 380 000 000 metres (380 000 kilometres).

Humans are about 2 metres tall. The metre is the standard measurement of length.

The earth is 12 000 000 metres (12 000 kilometres) across.

These sizes are in our "human scale".

1 centimetre

1 millimetre

10^{16}	10 000 000 000 000 000m
10^{15}	1 000 000 000 000 000m
10^{14}	100 000 000 000 000m
10^{13}	10 000 000 000 000m
10^{12}	1 000 000 000 000m
10^{11}	100 000 000 000m
10^{10}	10 000 000 000m
10^9	1000 000 000m
10^8	100 000 000m
10^7	10 000 000m
10^6	1 000 000m
10^5	100 000m
10^4	10 000m
10^3	1 000m
10^2	100m
10^1	10m
1	1m
10^{-1}	0.1m
10^{-2}	0.01m
10^{-3}	0.001m
10^{-4}	0.0001m
10^{-5}	0.00001m
10^{-6}	0.000001m
10^{-7}	0.000000 1m
10^{-8}	0.000000 01m
10^{-9}	0.000000 001m
10^{-10}	0.000000 000 1m
10^{-11}	0.000000 000 01m
10^{-12}	0.000000 000 001m
10^{-13}	0.000000 000 000 1m
10^{-14}	0.000000 000 000 01m
10^{-15}	0.000000 000 000 001m

The width of a human blood cell

Blood cell

About the size of the smallest objects we can see (0.1 millimetres). It is the beginning of the microscopic scale.

The thickness of the outside wall of a plant cell

About the size of the smallest thing which can be seen with an optical microscope.

Plant cell wall

About the size of the smallest object which can be seen with an electron microscope, about the length of a large molecule.

Model of atom

The width of an atom

Nucleus of protons and neutrons

Model of molecule   Atom

The width of a subatomic particle (proton or neutron), part of the nucleus of an atom.

Magnifying glasses

With a magnifying glass, objects appear to be about three to about ten times larger than their real size (this is called a magnification of about three to ten). On page 42 you can see how a magnifying glass bends light rays from an object to make it appear larger. You will be able to see more with a good magnifying glass than with a cheap microscope.

Printing

Gather together as many different types of printing as you can find. Use your magnifying glass to look at the letters and pictures. Try to see how they have been made.

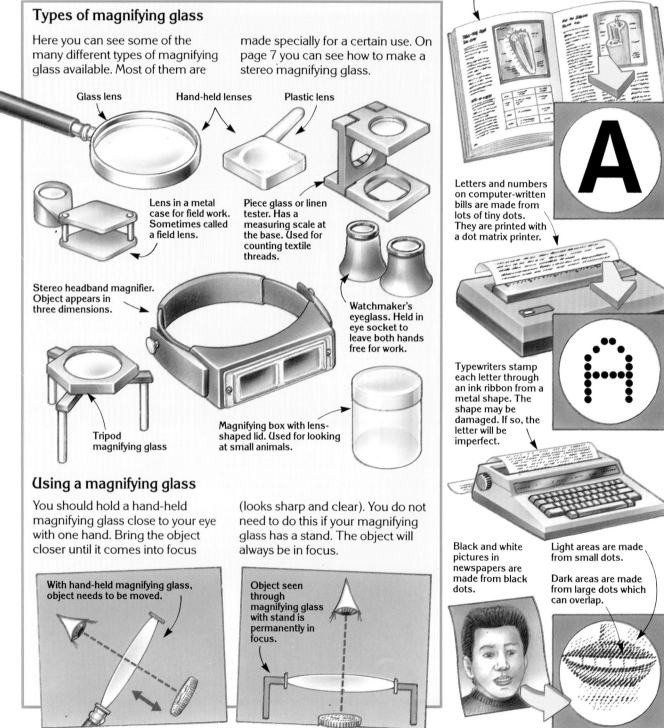

Types of magnifying glass

Here you can see some of the many different types of magnifying glass available. Most of them are made specially for a certain use. On page 7 you can see how to make a stereo magnifying glass.

Glass lens

Hand-held lenses

Plastic lens

Lens in a metal case for field work. Sometimes called a field lens.

Piece glass or linen tester. Has a measuring scale at the base. Used for counting textile threads.

Stereo headband magnifier. Object appears in three dimensions.

Watchmaker's eyeglass. Held in eye socket to leave both hands free for work.

Tripod magnifying glass

Magnifying box with lens-shaped lid. Used for looking at small animals.

Using a magnifying glass

You should hold a hand-held magnifying glass close to your eye with one hand. Bring the object closer until it comes into focus (looks sharp and clear). You do not need to do this if your magnifying glass has a stand. The object will always be in focus.

With hand-held magnifying glass, object needs to be moved.

Object seen through magnifying glass with stand is permanently in focus.

The letters in books and newspapers have very smooth edges. They are printed in ink.

Letters and numbers on computer-written bills are made from lots of tiny dots. They are printed with a dot matrix printer.

Typewriters stamp each letter through an ink ribbon from a metal shape. The shape may be damaged. If so, the letter will be imperfect.

Black and white pictures in newspapers are made from black dots.

Light areas are made from small dots.

Dark areas are made from large dots which can overlap.

Paper fibres

Collect together as many different types of paper as you can find. Tear a small strip off each to make a rough edge. Look at the surface and the torn edge with your magnifying glass.

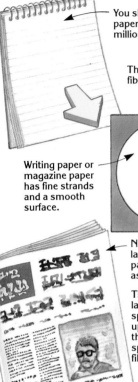

You should see that paper is made from millions of tiny strands.

The strands are fibres of wood.

Writing paper or magazine paper has fine strands and a smooth surface.

Newspaper has larger fibres. The paper is not as good as writing paper.

Tissue paper has large fibres which are spread out. It soaks up liquids because they flow into the spaces between the fibres.

Fibres and fabrics

Look at the fabrics in your clothes and other household things like furniture and umbrellas. Try to find both natural and man-made fabrics. Also find some different types of thread, such as cotton.

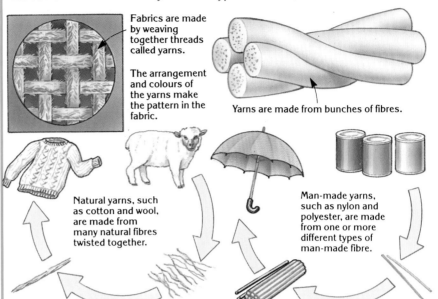

Fabrics are made by weaving together threads called yarns.

The arrangement and colours of the yarns make the pattern in the fabric.

Yarns are made from bunches of fibres.

Natural yarns, such as cotton and wool, are made from many natural fibres twisted together.

Man-made yarns, such as nylon and polyester, are made from one or more different types of man-made fibre.

Skin

Look closely at different areas of your skin using your magnifying glass. You will find different types of skin in different places.

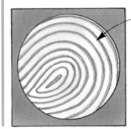

The skin on your fingertips is very sensitive and has many ridges.

These produce fingerprints (see pages 38-39).

You may see small pores between the ridges.

The skin on your arms is smoother and less sensitive.

Hairs grow from hair follicles under the skin.

Magnifying in stereo

Here you can find out how to make a stereo magnifier. With it you can see the depth of objects because you are looking with both eyes and can see in three dimensions. You will find it useful in some of the projects in this book.

You will need two similar magnifying glasses. They should be about 4cm wide and have quite a low magnification. Plastic ones are best because they are cheap and light. You also need a piece of thick card and some sticky tape.

Cut a strip from the card about 2cm wider than the magnifying glasses.

Make three bends in the card. Score the top side first to make it easier to bend.

Cut a hole to look through out of the middle. It should be narrow enough so that the magnifying glasses do not fall through.

The ends of the card should be high enough so that the surface under the magnifying glasses is in focus.

Tape a narrow strip of card between the uprights to keep them in place.

Put a magnifying glass over each half of the hole and use sticky tape to hold them in place.

Put the magnifier over the object you want to look at and look through with both eyes to see the stereo image. You can use a lamp to light up the object.

Types of microscope

A microscope magnifies an object many more times than a magnifying glass by using two lenses. The objective lens magnifies the object and produces an image of it. This image is then magnified by the eyepiece (the second lens) to produce another image, the one you see when you look through the microscope. See page 43 to find out how the lenses work. Optical microscopes can normally magnify from about 50 to about 1000 times, but 2000 times is possible.

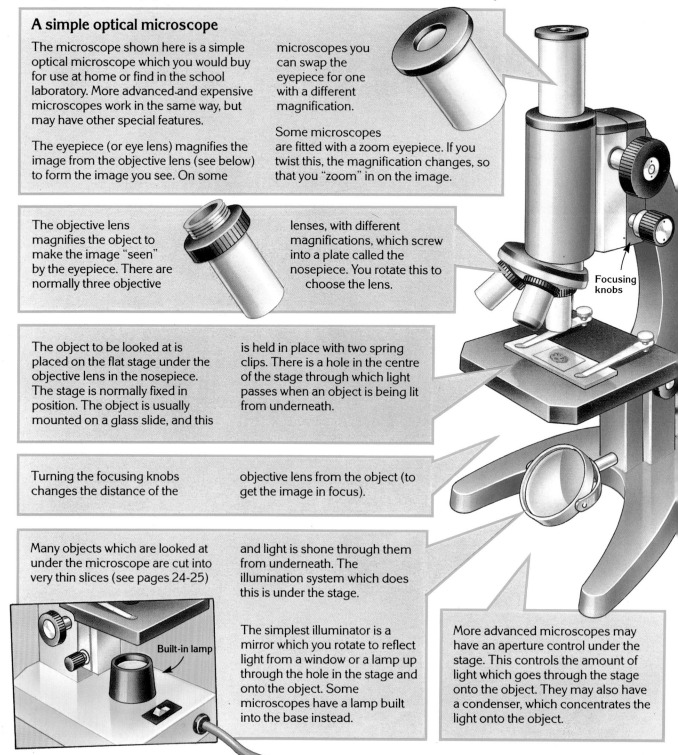

A simple optical microscope

The microscope shown here is a simple optical microscope which you would buy for use at home or find in the school laboratory. More advanced and expensive microscopes work in the same way, but may have other special features.

The eyepiece (or eye lens) magnifies the image from the objective lens (see below) to form the image you see. On some microscopes you can swap the eyepiece for one with a different magnification.

Some microscopes are fitted with a zoom eyepiece. If you twist this, the magnification changes, so that you "zoom" in on the image.

The objective lens magnifies the object to make the image "seen" by the eyepiece. There are normally three objective lenses, with different magnifications, which screw into a plate called the nosepiece. You rotate this to choose the lens.

Focusing knobs

The object to be looked at is placed on the flat stage under the objective lens in the nosepiece. The stage is normally fixed in position. The object is usually mounted on a glass slide, and this is held in place with two spring clips. There is a hole in the centre of the stage through which light passes when an object is being lit from underneath.

Turning the focusing knobs changes the distance of the objective lens from the object (to get the image in focus).

Many objects which are looked at under the microscope are cut into very thin slices (see pages 24-25) and light is shone through them from underneath. The illumination system which does this is under the stage.

The simplest illuminator is a mirror which you rotate to reflect light from a window or a lamp up through the hole in the stage and onto the object. Some microscopes have a lamp built into the base instead.

Built-in lamp

More advanced microscopes may have an aperture control under the stage. This controls the amount of light which goes through the stage onto the object. They may also have a condenser, which concentrates the light onto the object.

Magnification

The magnification of an image is the number of times larger it is than the object. Lenses of different magnifying powers give different magnifications. A microscope's magnifying power is that of the two lenses multiplied together.

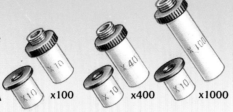

x100   **x400**   **x1000**

A microscope will normally have three objective lenses like this. They are called the low, medium and high power lenses.

More optical microscopes

Here you can see some of the different types of microscope available. Although they all look different, they work in much the same way as the simple optical microscope. You will find some other more specialist microscopes explained in different places in this book.

Binocular microscopes have two eyepieces to make viewing more comfortable. Both eyes see the same image (it is not in three dimensions, as with the stereomicroscope below). A multi-ocular microscope has two or more eyepieces so that more than one person can look through it at once.

Field microscopes are light and compact so that they can be carried around outdoors. They are used in field studies to look at objects which could not be taken back to a laboratory.

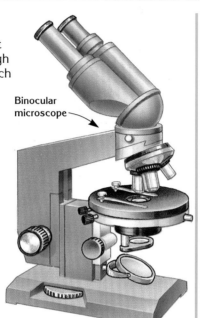

Binocular microscope

This simple field microscope has one objective lens and an overall magnification of about x50.

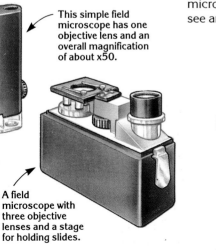

A field microscope with three objective lenses and a stage for holding slides.

A stereomicroscope consists of a pair of microscopes, one for each eye. The object is seen in three dimensions because each eye has a different view. The magnification is lower than in a normal microscope, but the images you see are much more spectacular.

Stereomicroscope

Accessories

A projector screen can be fitted so that the image you would normally see is projected onto a screen. This system is used for teaching, where a whole class can see the object.

Microscope with projector screen

A camera can be attached to a microscope in place of the eyepiece. Photographs of the object can then be taken so that a permanent record can be kept.

A video camera can be attached to some microscopes so images of moving objects (like tiny animals) can be shown on a screen and recorded on video tape.

Electron microscopes

An optical microscope can only magnify objects up to about 2000 times. Some electron microscopes can magnify up to about 250 000 times (for more about them, see pages 44-45).

Scanning electron microscope

How to use a microscope

Before you use your microscope, you need to know how to set it up properly. These two pages contain instructions for you to follow. You should come back to here each time you use your microscope, until you know the instructions by heart. As well as the microscope, you will need other equipment, such as slides and pipettes (there is a list on page 46). You will find out how to use these when they are needed for experiments in the book.

Where to set up your microscope

You will need a steady table to stand your microscope on. Position the microscope so that you can sit at the table and look down through the eyepiece without stretching or leaning over. Try to use a large table so that you have plenty of space for preparing slides and storing other equipment.

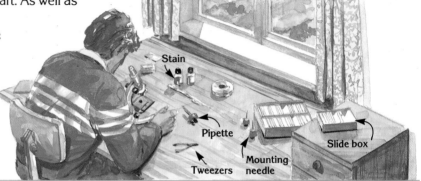

Stain

Pipette

Tweezers

Mounting needle

Slide box

Lighting

Any object you look at through your microscope must be well lit for you to see it in detail. The instructions below show you how to set up bottom lighting (or transmitted lighting), where the light comes from below and goes through the object (see also top lighting, page 13). Your light source can be a window or a lamp.

Most microscopes let you tilt the ocular tube backwards and forwards so that it is easier to look through it. If you can do this with your microscope, adjust the tube to a comfortable angle.

If you are using a lamp for your lighting, put it about 20cm away from the microscope. Adjust the lamp so that the light points towards the mirror under the stage.

Turn the nosepiece on your microscope so that you will look through the lowest power objective lens. This is normally the shortest one. If your microscope has an aperture control, open it fully.

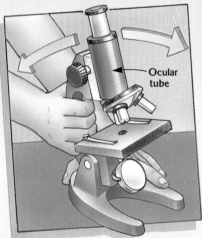

Ocular tube

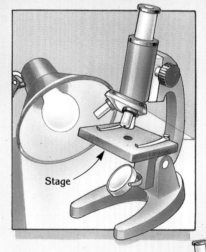

Stage

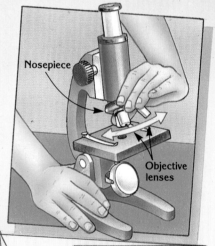

Nosepiece

Objective lenses

Look through the microscope. You should see a circle of light against a black background. Twist the mirror around to make the circle as bright and even as possible.

If you cannot see a circle of light, your objective lens is probably not in line with the ocular tube. Adjust the nosepiece until you hear the lens click into place.

Looking at a slide

The following instructions show you how to look at a microscope slide. You will probably get a ready-made slide with your microscope outfit which you can practise with. If not, put a few grains of salt or sugar in the centre of a clean, damp slide instead. You should follow the instructions below from the start each time you look at a slide, until you know them well.

Make sure you know which way you need to turn the focusing knob to make the lens move up and down. Practise raising and lowering the lenses.
▼

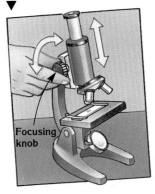

Some microscopes have what is known as stage focusing. When you turn the focusing knob, the whole stage moves up and down instead of the nosepiece.
▼

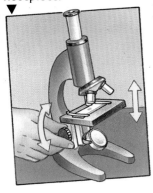

Turn the focusing knob to raise the lens as far as possible and turn the nosepiece to select the lowest power lens. Always start with this lens. It lets you see more of the object, so you can find the part you are interested in more easily.
▼

Put your slide on the stage so that the centre (the bit you want to look at) is over the hole and under the lens. Use the clips to hold the slide in place.
▼

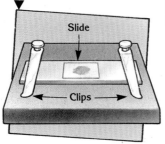

Look from the side with your eyes level with the stage. Turn the focusing knob to bring the lens down very close to, but not touching, the slide.
▼

Now look down through the microscope and slowly raise the lens by turning the focusing knob. At some point as the lens moves up, the object will come into focus (it will become sharp and clear).
▼

Now adjust the aperture control if you have one. Close it until the circle of light dims, and then open it again slightly. This will stop light from around the object getting in and spoiling the image.

You can slowly move a slide around to find the bit of an object you are interested in. The image will move in the opposite direction to that in which you move the slide. It is also upside down and reversed from side to side.

You can look at bits of the image in more detail with a higher power objective lens. Raise the lenses before selecting the new one, then re-focus, using the same steps as before.

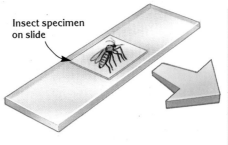

Insect specimen on slide

First microscope projects

On these two pages, there are some suggestions for basic things to look at with your microscope. These projects are quite simple and only need a little preparation. They will help you to get used to focusing your microscope and lighting objects in different ways. Remember to follow the instructions on pages 10-11. For some of the projects, you will need top lighting, which is explained on the opposite page.

Feathers

Find a white feather which is undamaged. Using a pair of sharp scissors, cut out a piece as shown in the diagram below. Trap it between two slides and use some tape to hold the slides together. Examine the piece of feather using bottom lighting. See if you can identify its structure.

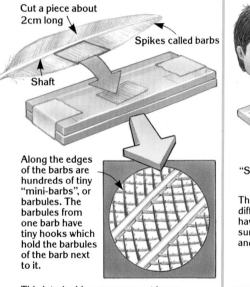

Cut a piece about 2cm long

Spikes called barbs

Shaft

Along the edges of the barbs are hundreds of tiny "mini-barbs", or barbules. The barbules from one barb have tiny hooks which hold the barbules of the barb next to it.

This interlocking arrangement keeps feathers in shape while a bird is flying.

Glass

Make a mark on a slide with a felt pen, put the slide on the stage and focus on the mark using top lighting. The surface of the slide should be in focus. Move the slide until you can see its edge.

You can see that the glass is not cut cleanly. It has been broken along a straight line.

Hairs

Take a hair from your head and put it on a slide. Hold it in place with two small pieces of sticky tape and look carefully at the surface of the hair. Try top and then bottom lighting. If you have any pets, look at their hairs in the same way. You can get sheep's hair from a pure wool jumper.

Human hair

"Scaly" surface

The hairs from different animals have a different surface pattern and shape.

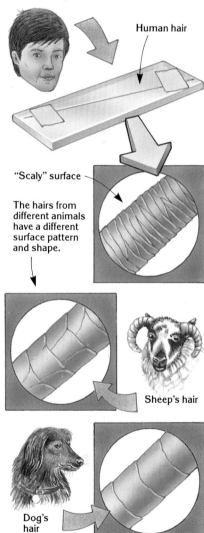

Sheep's hair

Dog's hair

See how many different hairs you can find.

Photographs

Find as many different types of photograph as you can. Try to include both black and white and colour negatives, prints and slides. You do not need to put them on a slide, just hold them on the stage with the clips. Use top lighting for prints and bottom lighting for negatives and slides. Try looking at the different areas which make up the picture.

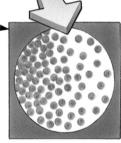

On black and white negatives, you can see tiny dark particles. They are formed from crystals which change when light hits them. This process records the photograph.

The colours on coloured slides and negatives have patches of three colours which form all the other colours.

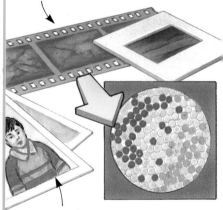

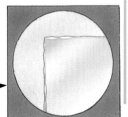

You will need your highest power objective lens and good top lighting to see the grains on prints. They are much smaller than the ones on the slides and negatives.

Dust

Scrape a small amount of dust onto a slide and examine it using top lighting. Look at the whole of the slide and try to work out what all the different bits are.

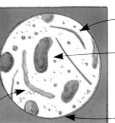

Fibres from paper and cloth

Household dust has lots of bits of dead skin in it.

Pieces of hair

In towns, there will be soot particles.

Top lighting

On page 10, you learnt how to adjust your microscope for lighting from under the stage. This type of lighting (bottom lighting or transmitted lighting) is used for transparent objects. Some objects are not transparent and will just appear as a dark shape if you use bottom lighting. They have to be lit from above to see them in any detail. This is called top lighting.

Aim lamp at object on stage.

You will need to move the lamp around to get the best lighting.

Light reflects from object into lenses.

Alter the mirror so that no light comes up through the stage.

Slides

Slides which you buy from a microscope shop are usually a standard size of 75mm by 25mm, and are about 1mm to 2mm thick, although slides from a microscope kit may be smaller and thinner. They are made of glass so that they can be used whether you are using top or bottom lighting (with bottom lighting, the light has to come up through them).

Types of slide

Plain slide

You can buy prepared slides from microscope shops. They already have specimens on them.

Cavity and ring slides for examining pond creatures in a drop of water.

Cover slips are very thin and easily broken. They are used to cover the object on the slide and help to stop it drying out. You can find out how to use them to make temporary and semi-permanent mounts on pages 14-15 and 36.

Drawing what you see

Making drawings is a good way of keeping a record of what you see through your microscope. Here are some tips which may help you. Make sure you are sitting in a comfortable position.

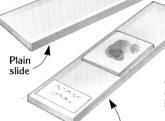

Look down the microscope with one eye and at your paper with the other.

Always use a sharp HB pencil.

Draw a circle first and lightly draw a grid over it. This will help you draw the details in the correct place and at the right size.

Give your drawing a title. Also make a note of the magnification you used, and the date.

A first look at cells

Most plant and animal tissue is made up of different units called cells. These were first seen by Robert Hooke when he looked at a piece of cork. Within each plant or animal, there are many different types of cell, each doing a different job. They are all important to the process of keeping the plant or animal alive.

Preparing cells

Normally, when scientists want to look at cells from a plant or animal, they cut off a very thin slice called a section (see pages 24-25).

However, you can look at plant cells from an onion and animal cells from your cheek without making a section.

On pages 30-31, you can find out how to stain samples to see them better, but you can start off by looking at them as they are. You should still see the main features.

Remove the brown skin from the outside of an onion and cut out a piece from a layer of the inside flesh as shown in the diagram. On the inside you will find a very thin, almost transparent membrane ("skin").

Peel this away using a pair of tweezers and make a temporary mount by following the instructions in the panel below. Look at the slide using bottom lighting (the cells will be almost transparent).

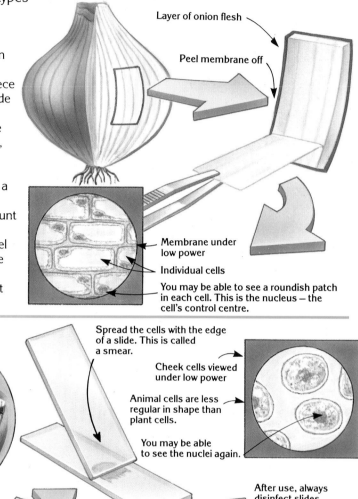

Layer of onion flesh

Peel membrane off

Membrane under low power

Individual cells

You may be able to see a roundish patch in each cell. This is the nucleus – the cell's control centre.

Lightly scrape the handle of a clean, disinfected spoon around the inside of your cheek. Carefully wipe the scrapings onto the centre of a slide and spread them out gently with the edge of another slide.

Leave the cells to dry, or dry them by waving the slide in the air, and then make a temporary mount. Examine the slide using bottom lighting.

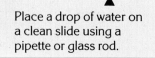

NEVER take cells from anyone's cheek but your own.

Spread the cells with the edge of a slide. This is called a smear.

Cheek cells viewed under low power

Animal cells are less regular in shape than plant cells.

You may be able to see the nuclei again.

After use, always disinfect slides, seal them in a plastic bag and throw them away.

Making a temporary mount

Most biological specimens have to be kept wet. Otherwise, they will dry up and decay. If the specimen is only going to be kept for a short time, a temporary or wet mount is used. You can find out how to make a semi-permanent mount on page 36.

▲ Place a drop of water on a clean slide using a pipette or glass rod.

▲ Carefully transfer the specimen into the drop of water.

▲ Pick up a cover slip by its edges and place one edge on the slide.

Cell structure

In the experiments on the left, you could see the outline of the cell and perhaps the nucleus. With higher power, you would be able to see more features inside cells. The pictures below show the main differences between plant and animal cells.

Animal cell

The nucleus is found in nearly all cells. It controls everything which happens in a cell.

The contents of the cell (except for the nucleus) are called cytoplasm. This can contain a number of special things.

Animal cells have granules of glycogen which act as a food store.

The cell membrane is a thin layer which holds in the contents (but lets liquids and gases through).

Plant cell

A cell wall is only found in plant cells. It is much thicker than the cell membrane and keeps the cell's shape.

Chloroplasts are found in plant cells. They make food from sunlight and make leaves green. Plant cells also contain starch granules which are a store of food.

Many cells have fluid-filled spaces called vacuoles. In plant cells, they are large and help to keep the cell's shape.

Special cells

You have seen that animal and plant cells are different by looking at onion and cheek cells. There are also many different types of plant and animal cell. These vary widely in size, shape and appearance. This is because each type of cell is specialized to do a certain job within the plant or animal. There are two examples below.

Specialized cells

Animal nerve cells carry electrical signals to and from the brain.

The fibre of a nerve cell can be several metres long in large animals like whales.

Cytoplasm

Nucleus

Pairs of guard cells on the underside of a leaf change shape to open or close holes through which the leaf "breathes" (see also page 27).

Cytoplasm

Nucleus

Cork cells

Robert Hooke was a 17th century microscopist. He examined cork and saw that it had a regular structure of units, which he called cells (see also pictures, page 4). You can see these cells if you look at a slice of a cork. Either just put a largish piece on the stage, or make a temporary mount of a very small piece. Use top lighting.

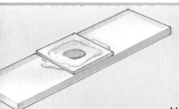

Lower the other edge of the slip. The water will spread out under it. Soak up any excess with blotting paper.

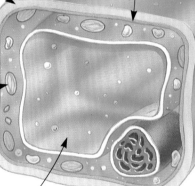

You may trap some air bubbles. They look like dark rings under the microscope. A few do not matter, but try again if there are lots.

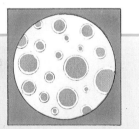

The cells are dead wood cells. Each has a cavity inside.

Cork cells

See page 27 for pencil wood cells.

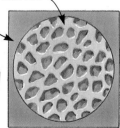

Simple organisms

On the next four pages, you can find out more about looking at very simple living things ("lower" organisms). They do not have the same structure of cells as true plants and animals ("higher" organisms), and are normally thought of as being neither plants nor animals.

Bacteria

Bacteria are very tiny organisms made up of just one unit, which is simpler than and very different to a plant or animal cell. They live and multiply anywhere they can find a source of energy to live on. Some live on or in other living things, either being harmful (causing diseases) or useful, for example, protecting against more harmful bacteria. Most bacteria, though, live on or in dead plants and animals and their actions cause decay (rotting). This is very important – see decomposing, page 18.

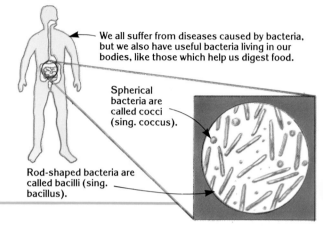

We all suffer from diseases caused by bacteria, but we also have useful bacteria living in our bodies, like those which help us digest food.

Spherical bacteria are called cocci (sing. coccus).

Rod-shaped bacteria are called bacilli (sing. bacillus).

Looking at bacteria

Groups (colonies) of bacteria can be seen easily with low power (a single bacterium is too small). Bacteria form colonies very rapidly (multiplying by splitting in two) as long as there is enough food.

You can grow colonies of harmless bacteria on jelly in shallow dishes with lids (petri dishes – see page 46). For about 12 dishes of jelly, you will need a vegetable stock cube and either a pack of agar (ordered from a chemist) or a standard (1 pint / 500ml) pack of gelatin or even a standard (1 pint) pack of dessert mix (if it contains a gelling agent like agar, carragheenan or guar gum).

Vegetable stock cube

Always be very careful with boiling water.

Gelatin or agar

Standard size petri dish

Dissolve the stock cube and 15g (½oz) of agar or all the gelatin or dessert mix in ½ pint (250ml) of boiling water. Simmer for 30 mins.

Sterilize the dishes and lids by boiling them quickly in water. Leave them in the water to cool.

Pour a shallow layer of jelly into each dish, put the lids on and leave the jelly to set. Then store the dishes upside-down until you need them. This stops water caused by condensation falling on the jelly.

Fingertip test

Press a clean, washed fingertip onto the surface of the jelly in a dish. Put the lid on the dish and leave it for a few days in a warm place. After this time, you should see pale whitish or creamy blobs (bacteria colonies) on the jelly in the outline of your fingertip. To look at these, you can either remove the lid and put the dish on the microscope stage, or cut out a sliver of jelly with bacteria on, and place it on a slide. Before you do anything, though, and as soon as you remove the lid, you must carefully dribble some disinfectant over the bacteria, and then leave this for a few minutes. When viewing, try both top and bottom lighting – top lighting will probably be best.

Slice of jelly placed on slide

Take care with knives and scalpels.

You should see one or more colonies. They may be different shapes.

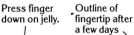

Press finger down on jelly.

Outline of fingertip after a few days

Bacteria grow where your finger left food for them.

Testing food for bacteria

Many different foodstuffs contain harmless bacteria. You can use your jelly to test for these. The test below examines flour.

First make some sterilized water. Put about 25ml of water into a small, clean bottle (like a cough medicine bottle) and put a loose cotton wool stopper in the neck.

Water level higher than in pan. Stops bottle falling over.

You may have to top up the pan with boiling water to stop it boiling dry.

Put the bottle in a pan of water and boil the water for about 1 hour with the pan lid on.

Allow your bottle of sterilized water to cool in the pan with the lid on before you use it. Add about 1gm of flour to the water and mix well.

Remove the lid from a dish of jelly and use a sterilized (boiled) glass rod or pipette to place some drops of the flour mixture onto the jelly, well spaced out in a circle.

Put the lid back on and leave the dish in a warm place for about 24 hours. If the flour contained bacteria, colonies will grow (yellow, white or possibly pinkish) in the places where you put the mixture on the jelly.

Look at the bacteria in the same way as before.

Yellowy bacteria colonies

Slice of jelly placed on slide

After use, always disinfect slides, seal them in a plastic bag and throw them away.

Different bacteria colonies

Now try testing some other foods. Most things can be mixed with water (mash small amounts of

more solid things). With things like dried fruit, soak them in the water, and then use the water.

Good things to look at

Canned foods (leave open for 24 hours first)

Milk

Oil

Yogurt

Dried fruit

Some of these may also develop fungi (see pages 18-19).

Honey →

Mustard

Viruses

Viruses are the smallest type of organism known to man. Some scientists think they are just complicated chemical substances, rather than living things. They cannot exist on their own, but instead they "invade" the cells of living things. They "force" these cells to make more of themselves (more of the virus). In this way, they reproduce and spread, causing many different kinds of diseases, ranging from colds and 'flu to killer diseases like AIDS.

Viruses were not discovered until long after bacteria, because they are too small to be seen with an optical microscope. However, scientists can now study them in detail with electron microscopes, and work out what they are made of. The scientists often make models to help them in their research.

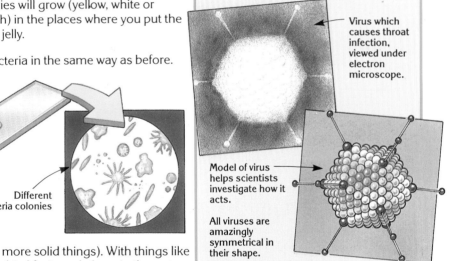

Virus which causes throat infection, viewed under electron microscope.

Model of virus helps scientists investigate how it acts.

All viruses are amazingly symmetrical in their shape.

Scientists grow viruses for study inside masses of living cells (in test tubes or bottles), which are kept alive and multiplying by giving them the right food.

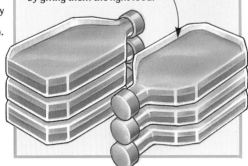

Fungi

Fungi are simple organisms, with no true cell structure, though they are more complex in structure than bacteria or viruses. They can be seen everywhere, for example, mould on bread or mushrooms in woods. Here you can find out how to look at them with your microscope.

Decomposing

Fungi cannot make their own food like green plants do. Instead, like bacteria, they feed on other substances, some on living tissue, but most on dead plants and animals. This is very important to all other living things. As they feed, the fungi and bacteria make the dead matter decay (rot). This is called decomposing. The complex chemicals in the dead matter are broken down into simple chemicals containing nitrogen and carbon. Once they are in these simple forms, the chemicals can be recycled through the earth, air and water. All other living things (plants and animals) depend on this recycling activity.

Plants need simple chemicals to grow. They make complex chemicals.

Animals need to eat plants (or plant-eating animals).

Decomposers cause decay of dead plants and animals. They return simple chemicals to the earth, air and water.

If simple chemicals were not recycled, no plants could grow, so nothing else could survive.

Decomposers act on our food in the same way as they act on dead matter in the earth – they break it down to simpler substances, making it "go bad". Sometimes, though, their action is used by man to produce foods.

All cheeses and yogurts are made with the help of bacteria, and blue cheeses have fungi growing in them. Bread and alcoholic drinks like beer are made using yeast – a very simple fungus which breaks down sugar into alcohol and carbon dioxide gas. Bakers use yeast because the carbon dioxide gas makes bread rise. Brewers use it because of the alcohol it produces.

Bread   Cheese

Yogurt

Wine and beer

If you put a ball of yeast in a warm sugar solution, you will see a froth appear after a few hours. This consists of bubbles of carbon dioxide gas. For more about yeast, see opposite page.

Looking at fungi

The basic make-up of a fungus is a hair-like part called a hypha. In most fungi, many hyphae twine together to form a mass called a mycelium, though there are also fungi with just one individual part ("cell"), such as yeast.

Fungi reproduce and spread by using spores – tiny particles which develop inside organs called fruiting bodies (see below) and are then scattered (normally by the wind). They land and grow on any suitable food.

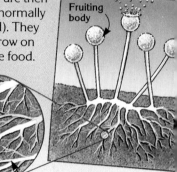

Fruiting body

Mesh of hyphae (mycelium)

You can easily grow different kinds of fungi to look at. Some good materials are suggested in the picture below – they should all be slightly damp. Fungi, mostly moulds, will appear on all these things after a few days. The common ones which grow on bread are called Mucor (white) and Penicillium (white with a bluish tinge).

Bread   Tea leaves   Straw

Soil

Penny-bun

Earth-star

Moisten a small piece of bread and put it in a dish. Leave it open to the air for a few hours, then cover it with its lid, or with a plate or glass. Make sure air cannot get in.

Keep it warm and look at it each day. After a few days, you should see a white mould with black dots, or a bluish mould.

Cut or pull off some of the mould with tweezers or forceps and make a temporary mount. Seal the bread in a bag and throw it away. Look at the mould with bottom lighting.

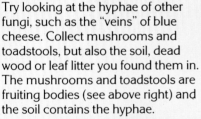

The "hairs" are hyphae.

The dots are fruiting bodies.

You could try to grow more hyphae on jelly (see right).

Try looking at the hyphae of other fungi, such as the "veins" of blue cheese. Collect mushrooms and toadstools, but also the soil, dead wood or leaf litter you found them in. The mushrooms and toadstools are fruiting bodies (see above right) and the soil contains the hyphae.

Using jelly dishes

You can grow your own fungi by using jelly dishes like those on pages 16-17. The ingredients for the jelly are slightly different. You should replace some of the water with orange or lemon juice and add a teaspoonful of sugar.

Use petri dishes as before.

Try pressing different fruit onto the jelly. Fruit bruises contain fungi, and the "bloom" (whitish film) on fruit like plums and grapes often contains yeast. You could also try lots of other food particles on the jelly, like a smear of jam or honey.

Plum

You should seal your dish with its lid and store it for about 48 hours, then look at the results in the same way as with bacteria (see pages 16-17), making sure to use disinfectant first. You may see fungal hyphae or yeast from a "bloom". You can store the dish and look at it from time to time to see them developing further, but be careful to keep hygiene standards high.

Groups of yeast "cells" look like milky blobs.

Cut a sliver of jelly or use a glass rod to take a smear. Make a temporary mount. You should see the yeast "cells".

Spores and fruiting bodies

The fruiting bodies of most fungi are quite easy to see with a microscope, but the spores are more difficult to view, though you could try bursting the fruiting bodies by pressing on the cover slip with a piece of blotting paper.

The best fruiting bodies to examine are mushrooms or toadstools. To look at the spores, place a cap on a slide, cover it with a cup or glass, leave it for about 48 hours and then examine the slide with a magnifying glass. You should see some specks – the spores. Make a temporary mount and view with bottom lighting.

Cap of toadstool

Remember – after use, always disinfect slides, seal them in a plastic bag and throw them away. Wash your hands thoroughly.

Different shaped fungal spores. Each different fungus will have different shaped spores.

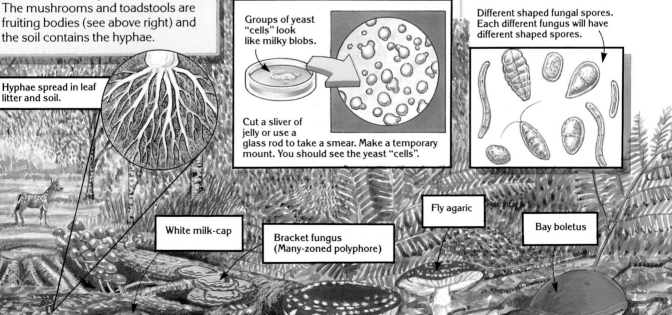

Hyphae spread in leaf litter and soil.

White milk-cap

Bracket fungus (Many-zoned polyphore)

Fly agaric

Bay boletus

Microscopic life in the sea

All bodies of water, from oceans to streams, contain a wide variety of life. Many of the plants and animals are so small that they can only be seen properly under a microscope. They are made of just one, or very few, cells. Here you can find out how to examine microscopic marine (sea) life and identify some of the thousands of different species. On pages 22-23, you can find out about tiny freshwater and soil creatures, and on pages 30-31, you can find out how to use stains to produce some of the colours shown here.

What is plankton?

Plankton is a term for all the microscopic plants and animals living near the surface of water. The plants are phytoplankton and the animals are zooplankton.

A litre of water may contain millions of plankton.

Phytoplankton use the sun's energy to grow. They are the basis of all the food chains in the sea.

Some large animals (e.g. some whales) just eat plankton.

Collecting marine life

You can collect marine life from the sea itself and from rock pools on the edge of the shore. You need some jars with lids to put the water in. You can use a plankton net (see page 46) to collect more animals and plants and add them to the water in the jars. Use other jars to collect sand and samples of the different growths around the pools.

Jars

Water from sea

Water from rock pool

Larger seaweed

Growths from water's edge

Sand from bottom of pool

Put labels on the jars showing where and when you collected the samples.

Looking at water samples

Put some of the water into a dish. Leave it for a few minutes, then take up a drop with a pipette. Put it onto a cavity or ring slide (see page 46) and put a cover slip over the top. Look at your sample for tiny plants and animals.

Try both top and bottom lighting. Top lighting may be best because some of the animals and plants, though transparent, will get lost against the background. Dark ground illumination (see above right) would be best of all.

Dark ground illumination

Most plankton are so transparent that they are difficult to see even with bottom lighting. Dark ground illumination is a special kind of lighting used to make them show up better. A special microscope attachment stops light coming from directly under the object, and only lets it come up from the sides. Only light which reflects off the objects goes into the objective lens. The plankton show up as bright objects on a dark background.

Dark ground illumination ▼

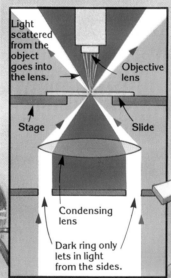

Light scattered from the object goes into the lens.

Objective lens

Stage

Slide

Condensing lens

Dark ring only lets in light from the sides.

Ring attachment from above

What you can see

Marine plants

Plants which live in the sea are very different from those on land. Most of them have no roots, leaves or flowers – they are called algae (there are also freshwater algae – see page 22). Many of them have only one cell and can only be seen with a microscope. Some are larger, like seaweeds, but still very simple.

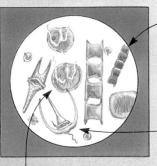

Diatoms are the most common algae in the sea. They are yellow-green and have an outer case of silica.

Dinoflagellates have two whip-like flagellae which they use to move.

This dinoflagellate gives off light to cause the phosphorescence often seen at sea.

Marine animals

There may be a great many different types of animal in your water samples, from simple, single-celled animals to tiny crabs. Scattered around the rest of this page are some of the types of animal you might find.

In summer there are many microscopic larvae and young stages of animals which live on the bottom or swim in the water, including crabs and barnacles, fish eggs and young jellyfish. You may also find tiny snails.

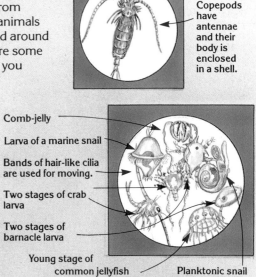

Copepods have antennae and their body is enclosed in a shell.

Comb-jelly

Larva of a marine snail

Bands of hair-like cilia are used for moving.

Two stages of crab larva

Two stages of barnacle larva

Young stage of common jellyfish

Planktonic snail

Rock pools

Most of the turf-like growths at the edge of a rock pool may look like mossy plants. Many of them may indeed be green, brown and red algae, but some are colonies of animals.

The water from the pool may contain more animals clinging to the weeds, and you should also be able to find free-swimming animals among the plants.

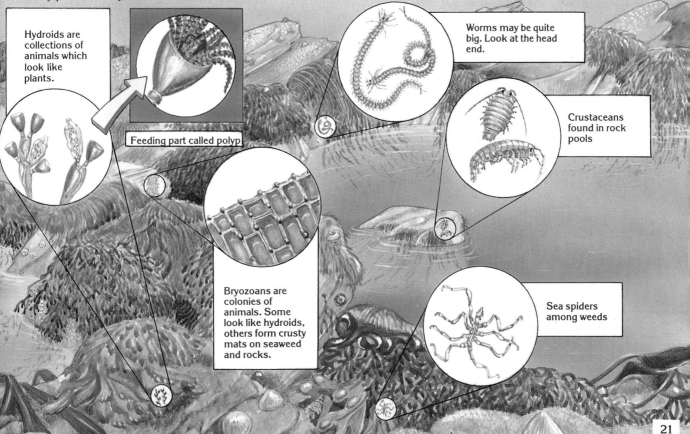

Hydroids are collections of animals which look like plants.

Feeding part called polyp

Bryozoans are colonies of animals. Some look like hydroids, others form crusty mats on seaweed and rocks.

Worms may be quite big. Look at the head end.

Crustaceans found in rock pools

Sea spiders among weeds

Microscopic life in fresh water

Ponds and lakes contain a wide variety of life. Some of the plants and animals are similar to those in the sea (see pages 20-21), but there are also different ones, only found in fresh water. Follow the same steps for looking at freshwater life under your microscope as for marine life.

Collecting freshwater life

You can collect microscopic freshwater animals and plants from ponds, lakes, ditches, slow-running streams and even puddles. Some plants grow on rocks at the bottom of the water.

Collect some water in jars. Put in some stones (with plant growths on), plants and mud from the bottom. When you get home, empty them into a larger jar and make some holes in the lid.

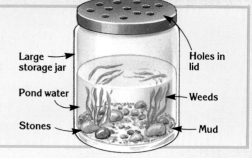

Large storage jar

Holes in lid

Pond water

Weeds

Stones

Mud

Freshwater plants

Algae are the simplest type of water plant, found in both fresh and sea water (see also page 21). There are lots of different types. Some you will only be able to see through your microscope (others include large weeds). Some form the green slimy growths on underwater rocks and the green slime on the surface of the water, others are the larger green masses on the surface. Look at samples taken from these different places. You should see some of the algae shown here.

Take drops of water from just under the surface. You should be able to see other tiny plants which are not filamentous like the ones on the left. They are not all green – many are yellow-green or blue-green.

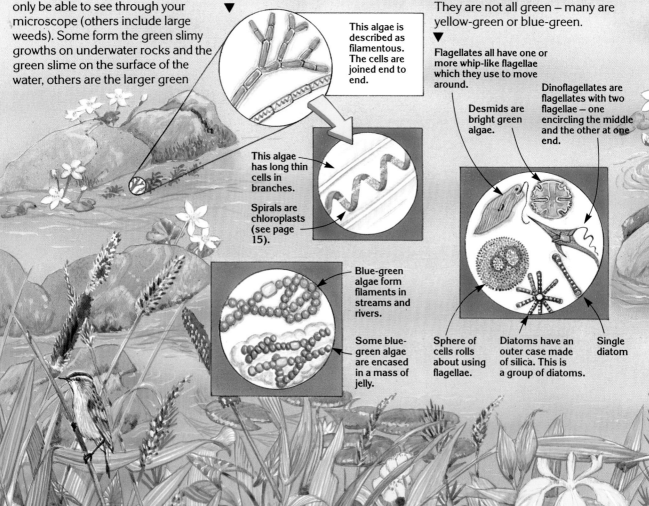

This algae is described as filamentous. The cells are joined end to end.

This algae has long thin cells in branches.

Spirals are chloroplasts (see page 15).

Flagellates all have one or more whip-like flagellae which they use to move around.

Desmids are bright green algae.

Dinoflagellates are flagellates with two flagellae – one encircling the middle and the other at one end.

Blue-green algae form filaments in streams and rivers.

Some blue-green algae are encased in a mass of jelly.

Sphere of cells rolls about using flagellae.

Diatoms have an outer case made of silica. This is a group of diatoms.

Single diatom

Freshwater animals

Millions of tiny animals such as those on this page, live in fresh water.

They live on algae and each other, and in turn are eaten by fish.

Ciliates are covered in lots of tiny hairs called cilia which they use to move along.

Rotifers have a foot, which they use to attach themselves to objects, and two rings of cilia on the head.

Some rotifers attach themselves to other animals. They often live in a tube.

Many animals live on the bottom of ponds or on underwater plants. They are often visible to the eye, but more detail can be seen with a microscope.

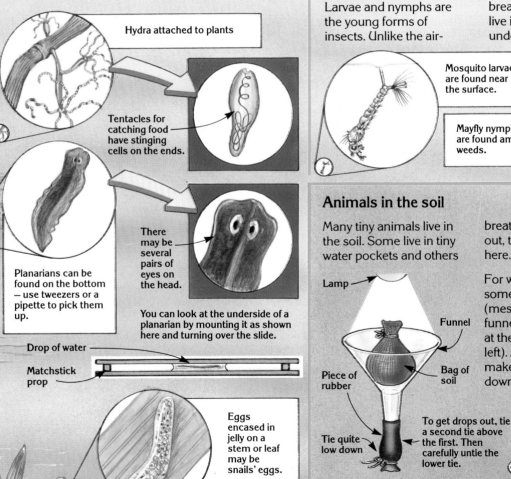

Hydra attached to plants

Tentacles for catching food have stinging cells on the ends.

Planarians can be found on the bottom — use tweezers or a pipette to pick them up.

There may be several pairs of eyes on the head.

You can look at the underside of a planarian by mounting it as shown here and turning over the slide.

Drop of water

Matchstick prop

Eggs encased in jelly on a stem or leaf may be snails' eggs.

Crustaceans have jointed legs, body segments and a hard outside skeleton. There are large ones, like crabs, and also microscopic ones. These include the young stages of larger crustaceans.

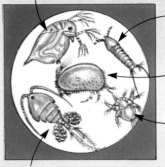

Cladocera (water fleas) have branched antennae.

Harpactacoids are copepods with long bodies and short antennae.

Ostracods (or seedshrimps) live near the bottom of pools. Their bodies are bean-shaped and completely enclosed.

When young stages of larger crustaceans are tiny (planktonic), they are called Nauplii.

Copepods have unbranched antennae.

Larvae and nymphs are the young forms of insects. Unlike the air-breathing adults, many live in the water or on underwater plants.

Mosquito larvae are found near the surface.

Mayfly nymphs are found among weeds.

Animals in the soil

Many tiny animals live in the soil. Some live in tiny water pockets and others breathe air. To get them out, try the techniques here.

For water animals, wrap some soil in a muslin (mesh) bag inside a funnel of water, blocked at the end (see below left). A strong light will make the animals move down into the funnel.

Lamp

Funnel

Bag of soil

Piece of rubber

Tie quite low down

To get drops out, tie a second tie above the first. Then carefully untie the lower tie.

For air-breathing animals, put the soil on a piece of mesh over an empty funnel. Put a container underneath.

Lamp

Soil

Funnel

Container

Piece of old strainer

Making sections

Plant and animal cells can only be seen properly with bottom lighting, but most are too thick to be completely transparent. To make it easier to see all the detail inside them, they need to be cut into thin slices, or sections, so that the light can pass through them properly.

To get the best results, the sections need to be just one cell thick. The best way to cut sections from a specimen is with a special device called a microtome.

Cutting sections in a laboratory

The three common types of microtome are shown here. Sections as thin as one thousandth of a millimetre (often called a micron) are cut for use with optical microscopes, but the sections for electron microscopes need to be thinner. They are cut with an ultramicrotome (see page 44).

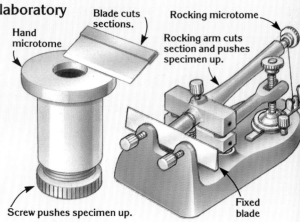

Blade cuts sections.

Hand microtome

Rocking microtome

Rocking arm cuts section and pushes specimen up.

Screw pushes specimen up.

Fixed blade

How to make a hand microtome

Using these instructions, you can make a simple hand microtome from easily available bits and pieces. You will be able to use it to cut quite thin sections, but you must be very careful when making the cuts.

The microtome is made from an empty cotton reel. Remove any labels (soak the reel if you need to) to leave a smooth surface.

Plastic cotton reel

Hole in plastic

Bolt goes through centre

You can use a block of wood with a hole through it, in place of the cotton reel. If so, you need a piece of plastic to go on the top (other end to the nut).

You need a bolt about 5mm in diameter and a nut to fit it. Glue the nut to the bottom of the cotton reel using strong waterproof glue and screw the bolt into it.

Make a thin, flat bar about 5cm long. It can be made from wood, plastic or metal. Glue it to the head of the bolt to make a handle for turning the nut.

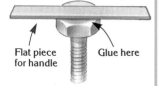

Flat piece for handle

Glue here

Marks help you cut same amount each time.

Make pen marks around the bottom of the completed microtome. Make a mark every 45 degrees to make eight marks altogether.

Using your microtome

Prepare your specimen first. It needs to be about 2cm long and should fit snugly into the hole in the microtome.

You need some other tools and materials before starting to cut your specimen into sections.

Carrot to be cut up and used to pack the specimen into the hole if it is not big enough.

New razor blade for cutting the sections. Look at the warning box before you use any razor blades.

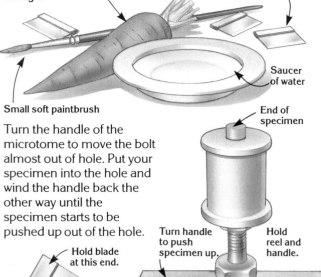

Small soft paintbrush

Saucer of water

End of specimen

Turn the handle of the microtome to move the bolt almost out of hole. Put your specimen into the hole and wind the handle back the other way until the specimen starts to be pushed up out of the hole.

Hold blade at this end.

Turn handle to push specimen up.

Hold reel and handle.

Wet the blade and the specimen with water. Hold the blade as flat as possible on the top of the reel and slice slowly across the specimen. Throw away the piece you have cut off.

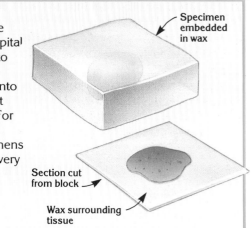

Specimen

Blade

Turning handle cuts section and pushes specimen up.

Rotary microtome

Some specimens, like living tissue from hospital patients, are too soft to be cut as they are. Instead, they are put into wax which is left to set and then sectioned. For more about this, see page 36. If the specimens need to be looked at very quickly, they can be frozen to make them harder, and then sectioned.

Specimen embedded in wax

Section cut from block

Wax surrounding tissue

Move the specimen up slightly (turn the handle), and make another cut. You should now have a section on the face of the blade.

The thickness of your section depends on the amount you turn the handle and the height of the thread on your bolt.

Gently sweep the section off the blade and into the saucer of water with the paintbrush. Cut a few more sections, keeping the blade wet all the time.

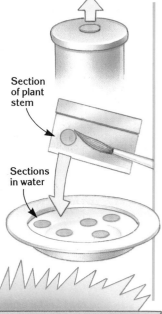

Section of plant stem

Sections in water

Looking at a plant section

Cells were first discovered when Robert Hooke looked at sections of cork (see page 15). By making sections of different parts of plants, you can see the many different types of cell they are made of. The next two pages show you some of these. Looking at plant cells has helped scientists work out how plants live.

Tulip stem

The stem of a plant is one of the easiest things to make into sections, because it is usually quite large and solid. A wide stem is best to start with, like that of a flower such as a tulip or daffodil. You could also try a leaf stem.

Cut a piece about 2cm long from your stem. Put it into your microtome and use some carrot to hold it tightly in place if you need to.

Make a temporary mount of one of your sections (see pages 14-15). You should see some of the cells shown here, though they will not be coloured. See page 26 for more about the different cells.

Cells in stem

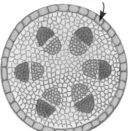

Warning

You will need a very sharp razor blade to cut the sections. Use a single-edged blade which you can get from a model or craft shop. Always make sure that the blade is facing away from you as you make a cut. Store your blades in a safe place to stop anybody accidently touching them. Put old blades in an old tin or jar and make sure it has a lid on it.

Looking at plants

With a microscope, you can see the arrangement and different shapes of the cells in different parts of a plant. You should make sections as shown on pages 24-25, make temporary mounts and use bottom lighting. The sections here have false colours, to show up the different cells to look out for. You can add colour and contrast to your sections by staining them (see pages 30-31).

Stems

You can find out how to prepare sections of a flower stem on page 25. The different parts of a stem are shown in this diagram.

A section cut across a stem like this is called a transverse section.

The outer layer of cells is called the epidermis.

The next layer in is called the cortex.

The pith is made up of all the cells in the middle of the stem.

Running through the stem are groups of cells called vascular bundles.

These groups of cells carry water and are called xylem.

These groups of cells carry food and are called phloem.

When you look at a tranverse (cross) section of a stem, like the one above, you see the cells end on. You can also cut sections along the stem. These are called longitudinal sections. To make a longitudinal section, first cut a transverse section.

Cut out a piece like this from a stem and put it into your microtome sideways.

Cells in longitudinal section

With high power, you can "home in" on different areas of the section.

These are long tubes of phloem

Roots

You can look at roots in the same way as stems. Roots from weeds, like chickweed, are quite easy to use, or you can grow some roots by putting a plant bulb in the top of a jar of water.

Transverse section of a root under low power (showing the whole section)

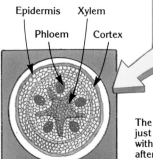

Epidermis   Xylem
Phloem   Cortex

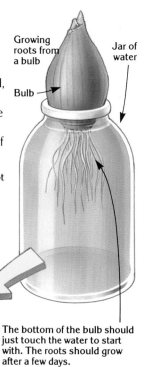

Growing roots from a bulb

Jar of water

Bulb

The bottom of the bulb should just touch the water to start with. The roots should grow after a few days.

Root hairs

Grow some roots from a bulb or take some roots from a plant you have dug up. If you look closely at them, you may see some tiny hairs. In order to look at the root surface and the hairs, make a longitudinal section of the root tip. Roots are very delicate, so be careful how you handle them.

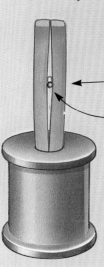

Cut off the last 5mm of a root. If there are no root hairs in this area, also cut a piece 5mm long from the area where the root hairs are growing, and look at sections from the two pieces separately.

Cut a piece of carrot to fit into your microtome and slice it down the middle.

Trap the root horizontally between the two halves of the carrot and cut a section.

Low power longitudinal section

Root hairs collect water and minerals from the soil.

This layer is the root cap. It protects the root.

New cells grow here and extend the root, pushing it down through the soil.

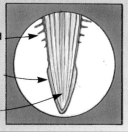

Wood and vegetables

At first glance, wood appears very different to soft stems and roots. If you look at it under a microscope, though, you will find that it has a very similar structure. The best wood to look at is from a pencil.

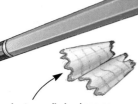

Look at pencil shavings or small pieces of pencil wood

You should be able to see tube-like cells. These are all closely-packed xylem cells.

You may be able to see part of the light and dark rings in the wood. In the light areas are cells which developed in the spring. The darker areas are made of cells which grew in the summer.

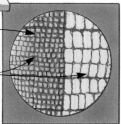

Many vegetables are parts of plants enlarged for storing food. They can be either roots or stems. You can find out which by looking at sections under your microscope and seeing how the cells are arranged.

Leaves

Leaves use the energy in sunlight to combine water and gases from the air into food. You can look at the inside of leaves to see the arrangement of the special cells which carry out these jobs.

Large leaves are easiest to make sections from. Try cutting a piece from the middle as shown. Put it vertically into your microtome and pack it in using carrot as shown. Make some transverse sections.

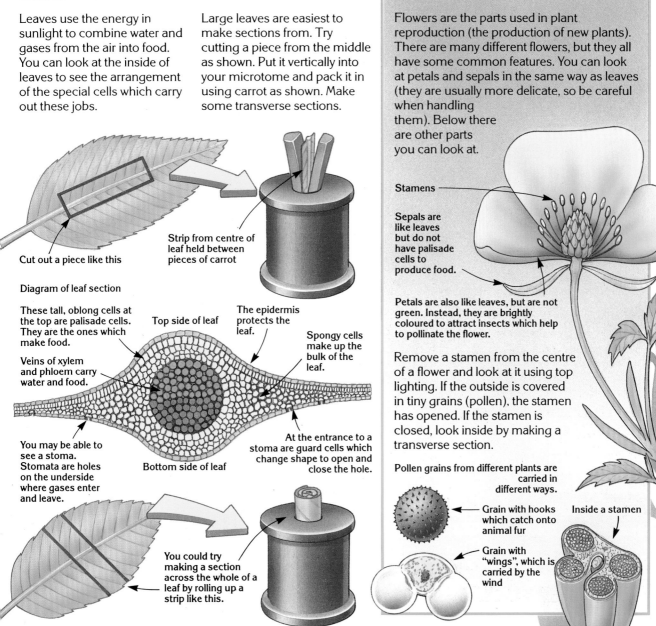

Cut out a piece like this

Strip from centre of leaf held between pieces of carrot

Diagram of leaf section

These tall, oblong cells at the top are palisade cells. They are the ones which make food.

Veins of xylem and phloem carry water and food.

Top side of leaf

The epidermis protects the leaf.

Spongy cells make up the bulk of the leaf.

You may be able to see a stoma. Stomata are holes on the underside where gases enter and leave.

Bottom side of leaf

At the entrance to a stoma are guard cells which change shape to open and close the hole.

You could try making a section across the whole of a leaf by rolling up a strip like this.

Flowers

Flowers are the parts used in plant reproduction (the production of new plants). There are many different flowers, but they all have some common features. You can look at petals and sepals in the same way as leaves (they are usually more delicate, so be careful when handling them). Below there are other parts you can look at.

Stamens

Sepals are like leaves but do not have palisade cells to produce food.

Petals are also like leaves, but are not green. Instead, they are brightly coloured to attract insects which help to pollinate the flower.

Remove a stamen from the centre of a flower and look at it using top lighting. If the outside is covered in tiny grains (pollen), the stamen has opened. If the stamen is closed, look inside by making a transverse section.

Pollen grains from different plants are carried in different ways.

Grain with hooks which catch onto animal fur

Grain with "wings", which is carried by the wind

Inside a stamen

Looking at insects

There are over a million different sorts of insect on earth and more individual insects than all the other animals put together. Here you can find out how to look at insects and their body parts (the same techniques can also be used for other "creepy crawlies", like spiders). You can look at live and dead insects, but do not kill insects just to look at them – you will find dead ones often enough.

You can find out how an insect's body is made up by looking at an insect like a housefly or a wasp with a magnifying glass. If you catch a live insect, you can look at it in a magnifying box like the one on page 6. You should be able to see all the different parts shown in the diagram below.

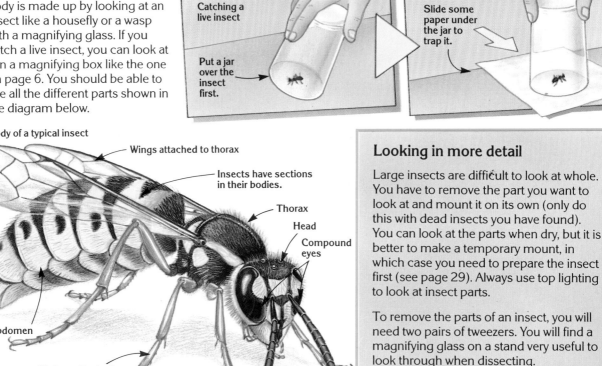

Catching a live insect

Put a jar over the insect first.

Slide some paper under the jar to trap it.

Body of a typical insect

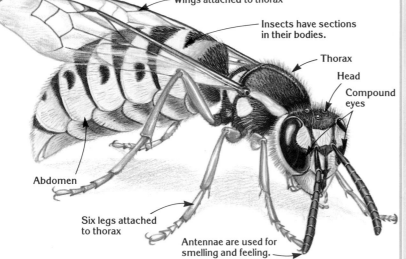

Wings attached to thorax

Insects have sections in their bodies.

Thorax

Head

Compound eyes

Abdomen

Six legs attached to thorax

Antennae are used for smelling and feeling.

Looking in more detail

Large insects are difficult to look at whole. You have to remove the part you want to look at and mount it on its own (only do this with dead insects you have found). You can look at the parts when dry, but it is better to make a temporary mount, in which case you need to prepare the insect first (see page 29). Always use top lighting to look at insect parts.

To remove the parts of an insect, you will need two pairs of tweezers. You will find a magnifying glass on a stand very useful to look through when dissecting.

Small insects can be mounted whole. Some insects look better mounted on one side than on their front or back.

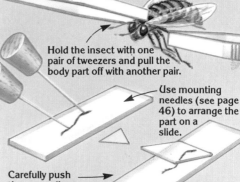

Hold the insect with one pair of tweezers and pull the body part off with another pair.

Use mounting needles (see page 46) to arrange the part on a slide.

Carefully push the cover slip down to squash the part.

If you want to make a semi-permanent mount, which lasts much longer (see page 36), you should soak the insects in clean water overnight after preparing them as shown on page 29.

Looking at live insects

Large insects are difficult to look at even under a microscope. They move about too much and are difficult to focus on. However, you can look at small insects, like ants, quite successfully with low power. Below you can see how to make a trap to keep them still while you look at them.

Making a slide trap

Cut a piece of thick card the same size as a slide (draw round a slide to get the shape).

Cut out a slot here. Keep the piece you remove.

Put a clean slide on each side of the card and a piece of sticky tape round one end.

Lift up the top slide and put a small insect into the gap.

Close the top and push the piece of card you cut out into the slot to trap the insect. View the insect with low power and top lighting.

Wings

Insect wings come in a wide variety of shapes and sizes. With most wings, you should use a temporary or semi-permanent mount and bottom lighting. Butterfly and moth wings are very delicate, though. They should be mounted dry and viewed with top lighting.

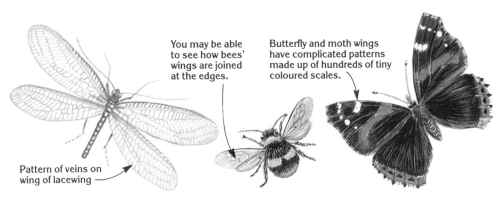

You may be able to see how bees' wings are joined at the edges.

Butterfly and moth wings have complicated patterns made up of hundreds of tiny coloured scales.

Pattern of veins on wing of lacewing

Legs

Insects have three pairs of legs. These have joints all the way along to make the leg very flexible. The shape of an insect's legs depends on how it lives. Some insects, such as beetles, have thick, fat legs and others have long, spindly legs.

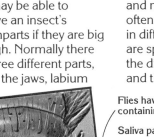

Legs of ground beetle

Some legs have claws for gripping.

Mosquito legs

Segments

Compound eyes

It is not easy to remove the compound eyes from an insect's head. You can look at them by removing the head and mounting it on its side.

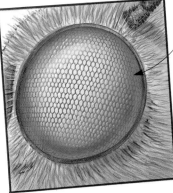

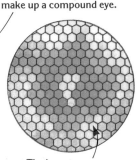

Hundreds of simple lenses make up a compound eye.

The insect sees a mosaic pattern.

Mouthparts

You may be able to remove an insect's mouthparts if they are big enough. Normally there are three different parts, called the jaws, labium and maxillae, but they often look very different in different insects (they are specially adapted for the diet of each insect and the way it feeds).

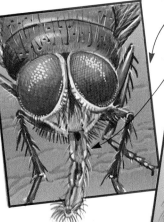

Flies have a large labium containing tubes.

Saliva passes down the tubes and dissolves the food, which is then sucked up.

Mosquitoes have long, sharp mouthparts which pierce skin and suck blood.

Preparing insects

You can soften insects by soaking them in washing soda solution for a few days. Pour 100ml of water into a jar and stir in 100g of washing soda. Put any insects you want to soften into the solution and leave them for a few days. Rinse the insects in clean water when you take them out. Always handle the insects with tweezers and wash your hands in clean water afterwards.

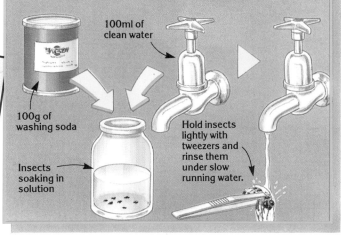

100ml of clean water

100g of washing soda

Insects soaking in solution

Hold insects lightly with tweezers and rinse them under slow running water.

Staining

Many things you look at under your microscope are quite difficult to see because they do not have much colour in them. If you use stains, they will be much more visible and you will be able to distinguish between many of the details inside them. Stains are most often used for objects viewed with bottom lighting (things which are transparent, or nearly transparent), especially sections or parts of plants and animals, or tiny, whole plants and animals.

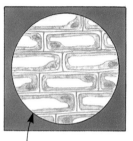
Basic microscope view of unstained plant cells

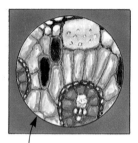
Elaborately stained plant cells from a laboratory section

Different stains

There are several basic stains which you can get hold of fairly easily. These are described below. If you have a microscope kit, it probably contains some of them. If not, most of them can be bought from large chemists or hardware shops.

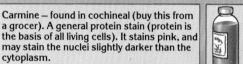

Carmine – found in cochineal (buy this from a grocer). A general protein stain (protein is the basis of all living cells). It stains pink, and may stain the nuclei slightly darker than the cytoplasm.

Acid fuchsin. Another general stain. It stains reddish brown and may stain the nucleus slightly darker.

Methylene blue "prefers" (preferentially stains) acids, so it stains the nuclei more strongly than the cytoplasm (nuclei are more acidic). It stains blue.

Eosin "prefers" alkalis, so it stains the cytoplasm more strongly than the nuclei (the cytoplasm is more alkaline). It stains pink.

Iodine – buy this as tincture of iodine from a chemist. It "prefers" complex carbohydrates (storage sugars found in all living things), so it stains grains of starch (sugar stores in plant cells) and glycogen (sugar stores in animal cells). It stains these different carbohydrates different colours, staining starch dark blue and glycogen red.

Using stains

Most stains are diluted ready for use. There are three basic staining techniques, explained on these pages, with different examples of things to look at. As well as the different stains suggested, you should try out all the others you have, to see what results they give. You should view all your stained samples with bottom lighting.

Dipping and rinsing

This technique is best for staining fairly solid pieces of tissue, like a piece of inner "skin" from an onion (see page 14) or a section of another root vegetable. It is also good for whole animals and plants, like plankton (see pages 20-23), and the more transparent parts of animals such as insects.

Place the sample in a small dish of stain. Use cochineal for the onion skin (you would also use this for plankton) and iodine for the other vegetable section. This should be something like carrot or turnip – potato is too starchy, and will take up too much stain. Leave the sample for about 3 minutes and then rinse it quickly by dipping it in a bowl of clean water (hold it

Drop the sample into the dish of stain.

Rinse it by dipping it quickly in and out of the water.

with tweezers). Transfer it to a slide and make a temporary mount.

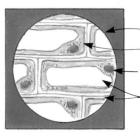
- Onion cells
- Light pink cytoplasm
- Slightly darker pink nuclei
- Clear cell walls and vacuoles (see page 15)

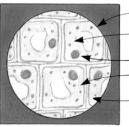
- Root vegetable cells
- Light yellow-brown cytoplasm
- Slightly darker brown nuclei
- Bluish-black starch grains
- Clear cell walls

Pulling stains

With very delicate samples, such as some plant sections, dipping is not ideal, as the sample may fall apart in the dish. You should try "pulling" the stain instead.

Take a leaf section and make a temporary mount. Use a pipette to place a drop of fuchsin on the slide next to one edge of the cover slip. Hold a piece of blotting paper or filter paper close to the opposite edge. The stain will be pulled under the cover slip and onto your section.

Excess stain pulled out onto paper.

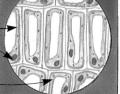

Stain pulled under slip.

Place drop next to one edge of cover slip.

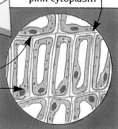

Plant cells (palisade cells)

Reddish-brown cytoplasm

Slightly darker nuclei

You may see chloroplasts (see page 15). If so, they may have a slightly green tinge.

With this technique, you can use a second stain after the first. With a new sample, pull some iodine under the cover slip. Then use a new piece of blotting paper to pull a drop of fuchsin or cochineal across. The excess iodine will be drawn off the sample, and the second stain will move onto it.

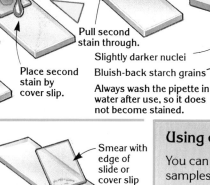

Pull first stain onto sample.

Place second stain by cover slip.

Pull second stain through.

Reddish-brown or pink cytoplasm

Slightly darker nuclei

Bluish-back starch grains

Always wash the pipette in water after use, so it does not become stained.

Staining smears

A group of cells spread onto a slide is called a smear. On page 14, you saw how to make a basic smear of cheek cells. You can stain these to give a better view. The most common use of smears is for looking at blood samples.

A mixture of eosin and methylene blue will give good colour contrast inside cells. Mix 50ml (2 fl.oz) of each in 100ml (3.5 fl.oz) of water, and boil for 20 minutes in a small bottle, placed in a larger pan of water (as on page 17).

Collect a cheek cell sample. Blood smears can be collected in the same way, using the handle of a spoon or the end of a glass rod. NEVER cut yourself on purpose – you will do it by accident often enough.

Smear the sample on a slide with the edge of another slide or a cover slip, and then allow it to dry. Place a few drops of stain onto the smear, leave for

Smear with edge of slide or cover slip

Drop of stain on sample

Be careful not to wash away sample.

Rinse with water.

5 to 10 minutes, and then rinse it under a slow-running tap. Leave it to dry out, then make a temporary mount and examine with bottom lighting.

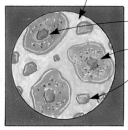

Cheek cells

Dark blue nuclei

Pink cytoplasm

You may see tiny food particles (stained pink).

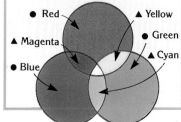

Blood cells

Many more red blood cells than white ones

Red blood cells stain all pink (they have no nuclei).

White blood cells stain pale pink, with dark blue nuclei.

Very pale pink plasma (fluid around cells)

Using colour filters

You can make your stained samples stand out better by using colour filters. You can get coloured celluloid or cellophane from a large stationers. Experiment by holding different coloured pieces below your objective lens, or you could attach them to the mirror. Filters with complementary colours to the stain should improve the contrast between different shades of the same colour.

Colours which make up white light

● Primary colours

▲ Secondary colours

Complementary colours are any two that produce white light when they mix (red and cyan, yellow and blue, magenta and green).

● Red   ▲ Yellow

▲ Magenta   ● Green

● Blue   ▲ Cyan

Rocks and minerals

Understanding rocks and minerals is very important in many industries, such as oil exploration and metal production. Geologists use microscopes to investigate the structure and composition of rocks, and you can do the same with your own microscope. For more about the mineral crystals which make up rocks, see page 35.

Collecting and looking at rocks

You will find pieces of rock almost everywhere. Small, flat pieces are best because they will fit easily under your microscope. Smooth surfaces, such as those of pebbles, are also good because they will not need much polishing.

Good places to find pieces of rock

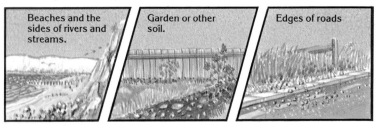

Beaches and the sides of rivers and streams.

Garden or other soil.

Edges of roads

Wash your pieces of rock in water. You can examine them as they are, but you can also polish or etch them as shown on page 33. You will not be able to mount them like other specimens. Very small pieces can go on a glass slide and larger ones on stiff card (which you put on the stage). In either case, hold them in place with some putty.

Press the stone firmly down into a blob of putty.

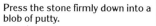

Slide

Try to arrange it so there is a flattish surface on top.

You may be able to see more detail if you wet the surface with a drop of water.

Use a dropping pipette

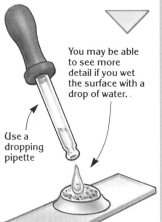

Warning

You will have to look at rock samples with top lighting. Be extra careful when focusing – the lens could be badly damaged if it hits the rock.

Types of rock

Rocks are made from crystals of minerals, which are complex chemical compounds. Different rocks are made from different minerals. You should be able to see the crystals using your microscope (some will be visible with a magnifying glass). Some common rocks are described below.

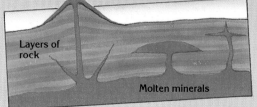

Layers of rock

Molten minerals

Igneous rocks are formed when hot molten (liquid) minerals from deep in the earth cool down and become solid crystals. The slower they cool down, the larger the crystals that are formed.

Interlocking crystals

Granite is an igneous rock which forms underground.

This colourless mineral is quartz.

The white or pink mineral is feldspar.

Black mica crystals

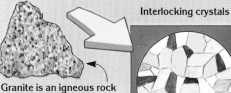

Basalt is also igneous. It forms on the surface.

Small interlocking crystals

Basalt may contain other coloured minerals.

Sedimentary rocks are formed from layers of particles which settle on the bottom of the sea, a lake or a river. They turn into rock because of the high pressure.

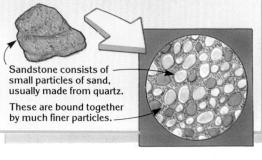

Sandstone consists of small particles of sand, usually made from quartz.

These are bound together by much finer particles.

Microfossils

Some sedimentary rocks contain the skeletons and shells of marine animals and plants (see pages 20-21) which lived millions of years ago. Many of these can only be seen with a microscope and are therefore called microfossils. Some rocks, such as chalk and limestone, are made only from these fossils.

You will have to break up rock pieces into their particles to find microfossils. This is done by soaking the rocks in chemicals. Clay, mud and shale can be broken up using hydrogen peroxide. You can get this from a chemist (you need 20 vols strength). Read the warning below before using it.

Clay, mudstone or shale

Hydrogen peroxide

Small pieces

Pour off the muddy liquid.

Remaining sludge

▲

Put some small pieces of rock into a jar of hydrogen peroxide for a few hours. You should be left with a sludge. Swirl this around and carefully pour off the muddy liquid. Add some fresh water, swirl the

sludge around and pour off the liquid again. Do this a few more times. Put some of the remaining sludge onto a slide and look at it. If you are lucky, you will see some microfossils.

Chalk or limestone

Vinegar

Small pieces

Sludge

▲

Other rocks, like chalk and limestone, can be put into vinegar. After a few hours, pour away the vinegar, add water, and repeat the process as before.

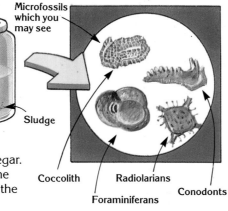

Microfossils which you may see

Coccolith   Radiolarians
Foraminiferans   Conodonts

Warning

Hydrogen peroxide will bleach your skin if it gets onto it. Always wear gloves, and read the instructions on the bottle carefully. To get rid of it, pour it into a large bowl of water and then pour this away.

Oil exploration

Oil and gas are formed from the remains of microscopic sea life which is compressed in sedimentary rock. The remains undergo chemical change because of the pressure and heat to form oil and gas. Geologists use microscopes to examine rock samples from deep under the ground (for more about this, see page 38).

Polishing rocks

You will be able to see more detail in your rock samples if you polish the surfaces to make them smoother. This is quite hard work, especially with harder rocks, but it is worth doing to see the surface particles of the rocks in more detail.

Rub the piece of rock against a larger one which is as hard or harder. Keep wetting the stone as you go. Examine the surface from time to time.

Use a circular motion when rubbing.

You can use fine grade emery paper to polish the sample further. Remember to keep adding water as you go. Keep examining the surface to see how you are progressing.

Lay the paper on a flat surface.

Polish the stone using a circular motion.

In laboratories, sections of rock samples are made which are thin enough for light to pass through. These are used for identifying the rocks. They are examined using polarized light (see page 35).

Etching

Etching is a way of producing raised patterns on the surface of a piece of rock using dilute acid. This eats away some of the minerals more than others. You can etch pieces of rock using vinegar.

Leave pieces of rock in vinegar for a few hours.

Put them on a slide from time to time to check progress.

Areas eaten away more by acid.

Crystals

Most natural materials which are not made from living substances are made up of crystals. The crystals of a substance have regular shaped sides and edges if they have been allowed to form naturally. Different substances have different shaped crystals. Large crystals are rare, but with a microscope you can see the tiny ones which make up many substances.

There are many different household substances which are in the form of crystals or are powders made from crystals. Many of them are suitable for looking at under a microscope. The easiest to look at are salt and sugar.

Put a few crystals of table salt or rock salt onto the centre of a slide and try looking at them with top lighting and then bottom lighting. You should find that top lighting is best because it makes the crystals look more solid.

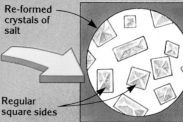

Salt crystals

Irregular shapes

You should be able to see that the surfaces are flat and the crystals were once cubes.

Salt particles from the kitchen look irregular because they have not been allowed to grow in their natural regular pattern, and have had their edges knocked off.

Look at crystals of sugar in the same way as you looked at salt crystals. Try different grades of sugar, such as icing sugar and granulated sugar. You should see different crystal shapes and sizes in different sugars.

Growing crystals

You can get crystals with much more regular shapes if you grow them yourself, by dissolving some existing crystals in water and then letting them recrystallize. The new crystals will be very small, but, seen under the microscope, they should have much straighter sides and sharper corners.

Drop a pinch of the substance into a teaspoon of warm water.

Leave the drop to dry.

When it has dissolved, smear a drop onto a microscope slide.

Re-formed crystals of salt

Regular square sides

Some liquids contain substances which form crystals. If the liquid is warmed up, some of it evaporates, but the rest forms crystals which are left behind.

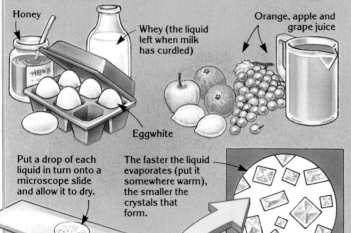

Honey

Whey (the liquid left when milk has curdled)

Orange, apple and grape juice

Eggwhite

Put a drop of each liquid in turn onto a microscope slide and allow it to dry.

The faster the liquid evaporates (put it somewhere warm), the smaller the crystals that form.

Inside crystals

Crystals form naturally in regular shapes because of the way the particles inside are joined together. The arrangements mean that the crystals grow with flat surfaces and can be broken along flat faces, called cleavage planes, parallel to these surfaces.

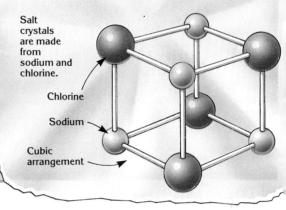

Salt crystals are made from sodium and chlorine.

Chlorine

Sodium

Cubic arrangement

Rock crystals

The particles in rock are actually crystals of the minerals which make up the rock. You can separate these crystals if you break down the rocks using the method on page 33. The particles can also be found in soil. Below you can find out how to clean soil so you can look at the particles.

Some shapes of mineral crystals in rock

Mica crystals are six-sided and usually thin.

Feldspar crystals are rectangular.

Quartz crystals are normally six-sided.

Preparing soil

Soils are a mixture of mineral particles from weathered rocks, together with plant and animal matter. Before you examine it, you need to clean the soil to leave just the minerals.

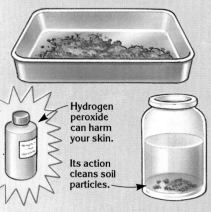

Collect some soil and spread it out onto a tray. Remove any particles bigger than about 2mm across. Let the rest dry completely.

Hydrogen peroxide can harm your skin.

Its action cleans soil particles.

Put about 10g of the soil into a jar and add 50ml of hydrogen peroxide (this is a dangerous chemical – see the warning on page 33 before using it). Leave it to stand for a few hours.

Add another 50ml of hydrogen peroxide and a pinch of sodium hexametaphosphate (get this from a hardware shop). Put everything in an old saucepan and bring it to the boil (stir as you go). Let it simmer for half an hour and then cool.

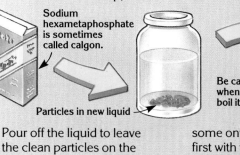

Sodium hexametaphosphate is sometimes called calgon.

Particles in new liquid

Be careful when you boil it up.

Pour off the liquid to leave the clean particles on the bottom of the pan. Spread some onto a slide and view first with top and then with bottom lighting.

Larger particles in the soil may be quartz. Collectively, they are known as sand.

The smallest particles you can see are silt.

Store the particles in a clean jar.

Polarizing microscopes

Many crystals are colourless, which makes them difficult to see with a microscope. Special polarizing microscopes are often used to make them show up.

Ordinary light is made up of waves which vibrate in many different directions. The waves making up polarized light vibrate in one direction only. Special polarizing material only lets through light vibrating in one direction, so it turns ordinary light into polarized light.

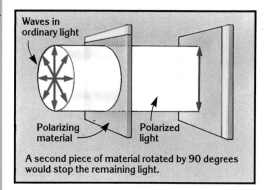

Waves in ordinary light

Polarizing material

Polarized light

A second piece of material rotated by 90 degrees would stop the remaining light.

Polarizing microscopes use two pieces of polarizing material, like those shown above. One is put below the stage and one above it. With no object on the stage, no light reaches the eye, because the second piece (the analyser) stops it all. When a crystal is put on the stage, different parts of it change the direction of the polarized light by different amounts, so the light is scattered. It passes through the analyser and shows up as lots of different colours.

The colours depend on the crystal and its thickness.

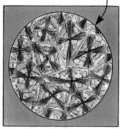

Polarizing microscopes are used by geologists to study and identify rocks and minerals.

A very thin, transparent section is cut from a rock sample.

Viewed with polarized light, the crystals show up in different colours.

The minerals can be identified from the colour and the thickness of the section.

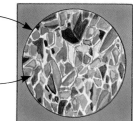

Mounting and measuring

Temporary (wet) mounts will not last very long, because the specimens will dry out and shrivel up. If you make semi-permanent mounts, your samples will last longer.

Making a semi-permanent mount

Instead of the drop of water used in temporary mounts, you should use a home-made jelly. For a basic jelly, you need gelatin, and for a better jelly, to make the mounts even longer lasting, you should use glycerine as well (you can buy both of these from a grocer). If you add a few crystals of the preservative thymol (from a chemist), your mounts will last even longer.

You will also need some gum arabic solution or some "size", and finally some enamel paint. You should be able to buy all of these from a model or craft shop.

Glycerine   Enamel paint   Gum arabic
Size   Thymol   Gelatin

Put 10g of gelatin and either 50ml of water or 25ml of water and 25ml of glycerine (for the better jelly) into a jar, with the thymol if you are using it. Sit the jar in a larger pot of hot water, and wait until the gelatin melts.

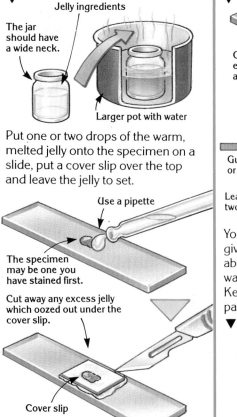

Jelly ingredients
The jar should have a wide neck.
Larger pot with water

Put one or two drops of the warm, melted jelly onto the specimen on a slide, put a cover slip over the top and leave the jelly to set.

Use a pipette
The specimen may be one you have stained first.

Cut away any excess jelly which oozed out under the cover slip.

Cover slip

The next step is to seal the mount. Put a layer of gum arabic or size all around the edge of the cover slip with a small paintbrush. Leave this to dry, then paint over it with one or two coats of paint.

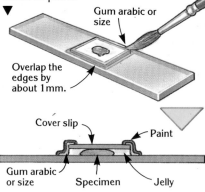

Gum arabic or size
Overlap the edges by about 1mm.

Cover slip   Paint
Gum arabic or size   Specimen   Jelly

Leave the first coat of paint to dry if you use two coats.

You should label all your mounts, giving the date and information about the specimen, such as where it was taken from and how it is stained. Keep your slides in a slide box (see page 46) so they do not get dusty.

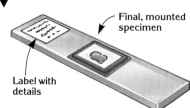

Final, mounted specimen
Label with details

Permanent mounts

Your semi-permanent mounts should last for months, or even a year, but will eventually dry out because there is still water in the specimen. When professionals make permanent mounts, they replace the water altogether, using a number of steps.

The first step is to soak the specimen in a fixative (see page 47). Then the water in the specimen is replaced by wax, and it is embedded in wax and sectioned. The water is then put back in, so the sections can be stained. Finally, the water is replaced by a mountant, which is left to set. This is a mixture of resin (a wax-like substance) and a type of plastic.

Measuring with a microscope

It is quite easy to measure the size of objects under the microscope. You can get a rough guide by holding a ruler next to your object, with the end piece in view (use a ruler where the end piece divides down as far as ½ millimetres).

You could also try finely tracing the ½ ruler scale onto good quality (very transparent) tracing paper or clear film, and put this under or next to the specimen.

The scale is magnified by the same amount as the object, so the sizes are correct for "real size".

The best way to get really accurate measurements, though, is to use two pieces of equipment called an eyepiece graticule and a stage micrometer. If you have a microscope kit, these may have been supplied with it. Otherwise, you can buy them from a specialist microscope shop.

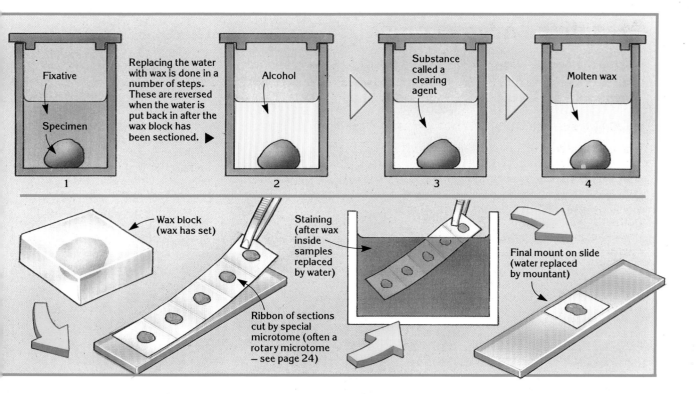

Fixative

Specimen

Replacing the water with wax is done in a number of steps. These are reversed when the water is put back in after the wax block has been sectioned. ▶

Alcohol

Substance called a clearing agent

Molten wax

1

2

3

4

Wax block (wax has set)

Staining (after wax inside samples replaced by water)

Final mount on slide (water replaced by mountant)

Ribbon of sections cut by special microtome (often a rotary microtome — see page 24)

An eyepiece graticule is a piece of clear film or glass which fits inside the eyepiece of a microscope (unscrew the very top piece and drop the graticule down inside). There are many different kinds, but they all have some kind of pattern of ruled lines on them.

For measuring things as shown here, you just need a simple graticule which has a ruled, graduated line marked on it. The graduation marks need not be numbered, and the actual measurement of the distance between them is not needed either.

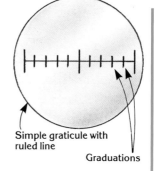

Simple graticule with ruled line

Graduations

A stage micrometer is an ordinary slide which has a ruled scale marked or etched on it. Unlike the graticule, the distance between the graduations is given, so it is a proper scale. The kind of micrometer you can buy has a line which is typically 10mm long, but the divisions marked by the graduations may vary from tenths to hundredths of a millimetre.

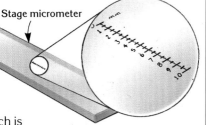

Stage micrometer

To measure the size of an object, first insert the eyepiece graticule and then look through your microscope. The graticule scale will be superimposed in focus over the top of the object, and you can work out how many units long it is.

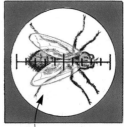

Object is 8 units long

Next, take away the object and put the micrometer on the stage. Now you can work out the length of the object by measuring the length of the correct number of units.

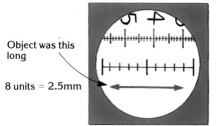

Object was this long

8 units = 2.5mm

The graticule image stays the same size if you alter the strength of the objective lens, but the magnification of the stage micrometer will change, just like that of the object.

Other graticules have grids on them and are used for counting objects.

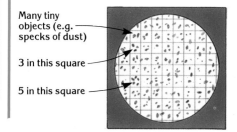

Many tiny objects (e.g. specks of dust)

3 in this square

5 in this square

Uses of the microscope

Modern optical and electron microscopes have a number of important uses in scientific research and industry. On the next four pages, you can find out more about some of these uses.

Medicine

The invention of the microscope led to enormous advances in the world of medicine. For example, bacteria were discovered, which meant medical scientists found out the causes of many illnesses and were able to develop cures for them.

Human tissue could also be examined closely for the first time, so scientists were able to work out exactly how our bodies work.

Optical microscopes are now used all the time in medicine. Doctors use them in hospital laboratories, when examining human tissue for disease. They also use microscopes when carrying out tricky operations, called microsurgery. Electron microscopes are used in research, for example when scientists are trying to work out the structure of viruses.

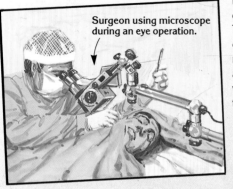
Surgeon using microscope during an eye operation.

This virus causes measles (it is shown in unrealistic colours).

Geology

Geologists examine pieces of rock under the microscope to find out what they are made from (see also pages 32-33).

In the oil industry, for example, rock samples from different levels are examined while a well is being drilled. This helps the oil company decide how the drilling should proceed. The rock samples can also give the geologists a lot of information about underground rock formations. This is important for drilling other wells in the same area.

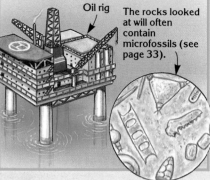
Oil rig

The rocks looked at will often contain microfossils (see page 33).

Forensic science

Microscopes play a vital role in helping detectives solve crimes. Magnifying glasses are often used at the scene of a crime, but all the fragments of evidence which are found are then taken away to be looked at under optical microscopes in the forensic science laboratory.

Detectives collect tiny pieces of evidence found at the scene of a crime, such as a burglary. They collect things like hairs, dirt from shoes, scraps of clothing, spots of blood, carpet fibres, and maybe glass from a broken window.

In the forensic science laboratory, slides are prepared and all the different things are examined under a microscope. So much detail can be seen that it often makes each type of particle, such as a type of fibre, unique. If the same type of particle is found on a suspect, it will be very important evidence in the case for charging them with the crime.

Detectives also take fingerprints. They work out which ones should not be there by eliminating the fingerprints of the people who live in the house. You can make your own library of "known" fingerprints, to compare with ones you find.

A fingerprint library

You will need a stamp pad. You can buy these from a stationer, or you can make your own by folding a soft cloth or some kitchen paper a number of times and then soaking it in poster paint. Take your own prints, as shown here, and also those of your family and friends. Ideally, you should take a full set of prints (10 prints) from each person.

What you will need

Paint pad or stamp pad

Pieces of paper

Slides

Scrapbook

Roll the finger several times from side to side on the pad.

Make a print by rolling the finger from side to side again on a scrapbook page, a small piece of paper or a slide (see right).

Push down quite hard.

Paper taped onto slides

Magnifying glass

If you just want to look at your prints with a magnifying glass, you can roll your finger directly onto the paper in a scrapbook. If you want to use your microscope, make prints on small pieces of paper, and tape these to slides. You could also try making the prints on glass slides.

Use low power, with top lighting for prints on paper and bottom lighting for prints on glass.

Make sure the slides are clean

Arch	Loop	Whorl	Delta	Island	Fork

Look closely at the prints and identify the different features (see right). Later, when you find an unidentified print, you should compare its features with those on your "known" prints.

Finding fingerprints

The most likely places to find prints around the house are doorknobs, switches and handles. Think about where else people put their hands. Smooth, polished surfaces show the best prints.

Scatter either talcum powder or finely ground, soft pencil lead (graphite) on and around the print. Use talcum powder on dark surfaces and graphite on light ones.

Talcum powder

Use a soft paintbrush to brush the powder gently over the print. Brush away any loose powder. You should see a clear print on the surface.

Stick a piece of wide sticky tape over the print, rub over the area with a fingernail or paperclip and then gently lift the tape. The print should transfer to the tape.

Stick the tape down on some paper (dark paper if you used talcum powder) or a slide. Now compare features with prints you know.

Tape stuck down on dark paper

You could also build up slide or scrapbook libraries of hairs and other fibres (e.g from clothing and carpets). You can then use your library to identify unknown fibres.

Uses of the microscope

Materials research and industry

Microscopes, both optical and electron, are used by scientists whose work involves testing different materials. Lots of tests are carried out, such as tests to see how much stress a material will take before it breaks.

The material may be stretched, squashed, heated or cooled, and is then looked at under the microscope to see if its structure has changed. Scientists also test to see how new materials react to chemicals, for example, how a new man-made fibre reacts to different detergents.

Special microscopes are often used for looking at shiny metals (and rocks). The light is directed down the ocular tube, and bounces off the metal straight back up the tube.

– Special light attachment

Some microscopes used to look at metals may have a hot stage. The stage heats up and cools the metal, so the effects of temperature can be studied actually while they are happening.

Microscopes are also used to check finished products for faults, such as cracks, before they are sold. This is called quality control. Also, when a product or piece of machinery fails, a microscope is often used in the investigation.

Look at different metals under your microscope, to check for "wear and tear". Use medium or low power and top lighting. You may see worn edges, or tiny cracks at points of particular stress.

Be careful with sharp edges

Tools

Needles

Cutlery

Nails

Keys

Pen nibs

In some industries, microscopes are needed in the actual process of production, because the things being made are so small. When gemstones are being cut or inspected, for example, the craftsman needs to look at them through a microscope. Another good example is the electronics industry.

Aeroplane crashes, for example, may be caused by metal fatigue, when tiny cracks appear in metal and get bigger because of vibration. Fragments from a crashed plane may show up metal fatigue when examined.

Worn edge of knife blade

Many modern electronic circuits, e.g. in wristwatches or computers, are microscopic.

Archaeology

Optical and electron microscopes help archaeologists build up a picture of how people lived long ago. Tiny things found at an archaeological dig are examined for clues. For example, certain features of animal bones found in ancient human settlements tell archaeologists whether the animals were wild or domesticated, which shows whether the people were hunters or farmers. Preserved grain shows that land was farmed with particular crops and preserved pollen also helps in working out the picture. Different types of pollen show the different plants which grew in a particular area.

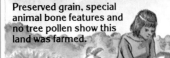

Preserved grain, special animal bone features and no tree pollen show this land was farmed.

Lots of tree pollen shows this area was a forest.

Food and the environment

The microscope is used widely to help farmers and people who package and store food. For example, it is used to investigate the bacteria and other parasites which cause animal deaths or crop failures.

The fight to produce more food also involves microscopes. Careful dissection of particular parts of a plant under a microscope lead to the development of new, faster growing strains of food plants and virus-free versions of plants.

Dissecting out healthy plant cells using a stereomicroscope

The cells are then grown in jelly, and produce a virus-free plant.

The preservation of food (treating it so it can be kept for longer) is carried out in a number of ways, such as cooking the food and then canning or bottling it, or pickling, freezing or drying it. In all cases, samples of the food are checked under a microscope at regular intervals to make sure that no tiny organisms have crept in (such as bacteria or fungal spores – see pages 16-19).

Scientists analyse the levels of different particles in the air, soil and water under a microscope to find out about pollution. See what is in your air by leaving a jelly dish (see page 16) or some strips of sticky tape out in the open for about 24 hours. Stretch the tape round a frame of some kind.

Frame (could be wood or stiff cardboard)

Strips of tape, sticky side outwards, facing the wind.

Weight it down with bricks or stones if necessary.

Jelly dish

Cut out a sliver of jelly or a piece of tape with specks on it and put it on a slide (sticky side up, if tape). Put a drop of water on it. Then put a cover slip over the top and look at the particles using bottom lighting and fairly high power.

What you see depends on the area you live in, and the time of year.

Pollen is found almost everywhere (grass pollen mainly in towns, all sorts of pollen in the country). This causes hay fever.

There will be lots of soot particles in town air.

Fungal spores

You may have caught tiny insects.

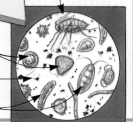

Archaeologists also look at preserved fibres, to show what people wore, as well as fragments of ancient buildings, pottery and tools. Archaeologists can often create a very detailed picture of how the people and their homes must have looked, from closely examining all the different materials and the way they were put together.

A cloth fragment may prove the people could weave. A piece of bone may show signs of sharpening for use as a tool.

Houses can sometimes be reconstructed after close examination of tiny fragments.

How an optical microscope works

In order to find out how an optical microscope works, you first need to understand how lenses "bend" light. This is called refraction. The single lens in a magnifying glass and the two lenses in an optical microscope all refract light to form the image you see.

Refraction

Light rays always travel through a substance (such as air) in a straight line, but if they go into a second kind of substance (such as water), and hit the border between the two substances at an angle, they are "bent", or refracted.

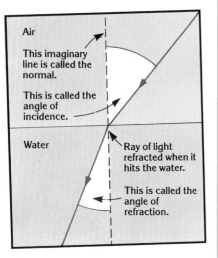

Air

This imaginary line is called the normal.

This is called the angle of incidence.

Water

Ray of light refracted when it hits the water.

This is called the angle of refraction.

You can see this for yourself if you put a stick into water at an angle. The stick will appear to be bent, and you will see it in the wrong place. This is because the eye always "thinks" light travels in a straight line.

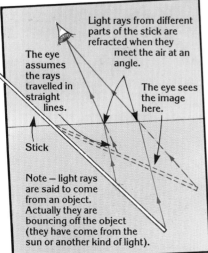

Light rays from different parts of the stick are refracted when they meet the air at an angle.

The eye assumes the rays travelled in straight lines.

The eye sees the image here.

Stick

Note — light rays are said to come from an object. Actually they are bouncing off the object (they have come from the sun or another kind of light).

Lenses and images

Like water, glass refracts light. Lenses are special pieces of glass, made with curved surfaces. They produce images of objects. An image is a view of an object at a place other than where the object is. Different shaped lenses produce different kinds of images, depending on the shape of the lens and the size and position of the object.

Types of lens

Convex			
	Bi-convex (both surfaces curve outwards)	Plano-convex (one surface curves outwards, the other is straight)	Convex meniscus (one surface curves outwards, the other inwards, but the lens is thicker in the middle than at the edges)
Concave	Bi-concave (both surfaces curve inwards)	Plano-concave (one surface curves inwards, the other is straight)	Concave meniscus (one surface curves inwards, the other outwards, but the lens is thicker at the edges than in the middle)

A magnifying glass has a single lens. This produces an image which is larger than the object (a magnified image).

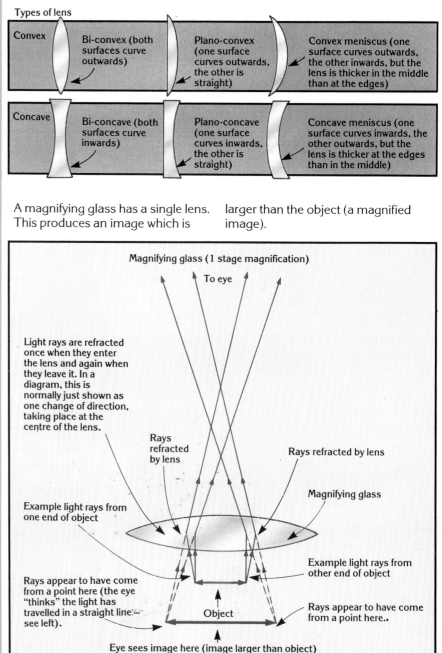

Magnifying glass (1 stage magnification)

To eye

Light rays are refracted once when they enter the lens and again when they leave it. In a diagram, this is normally just shown as one change of direction, taking place at the centre of the lens.

Rays refracted by lens

Rays refracted by lens

Magnifying glass

Example light rays from one end of object

Example light rays from other end of object

Rays appear to have come from a point here (the eye "thinks" the light has travelled in a straight line – see left).

Object

Rays appear to have come from a point here..

Eye sees image here (image larger than object)

In an optical microscope, there are two images, both magnified. The first is formed by the objective lens.

This acts as the object for the eyepiece (lens), which produces a second, even larger, image.

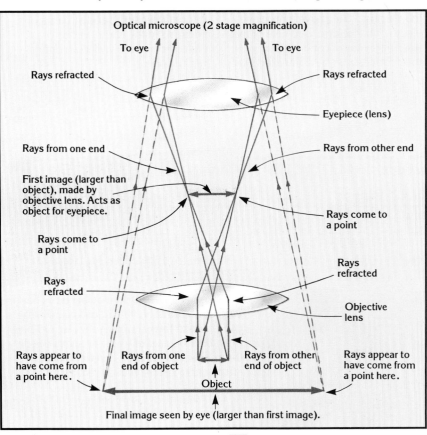

Optical microscope (2 stage magnification)

To eye
To eye

Rays refracted
Rays refracted

Eyepiece (lens)

Rays from one end
Rays from other end

First image (larger than object), made by objective lens. Acts as object for eyepiece.

Rays come to a point

Rays come to a point

Rays refracted

Rays refracted

Objective lens

Rays appear to have come from a point here.
Rays from one end of object
Rays from other end of object
Rays appear to have come from a point here.

Object

Final image seen by eye (larger than first image).

Compound lenses

The diagram above shows the lenses in an optical microscope as single bi-convex lenses. In fact, at least one of them, normally the objective lens, is a compound lens. This is a combination of two or more lenses of different types of glass.

Single lenses suffer from defects, which lead to the images being distorted in some way. One common problem is chromatic aberration. This is where the image has a "halo"

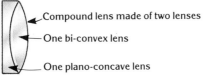

Compound lens made of two lenses
One bi-convex lens
One plano-concave lens

of colours around it, because the colours which make up white light have not all been refracted by the same amount.

A compound lens solves this and other problems – any distortion caused by one of its lenses is corrected by the other lens(es).

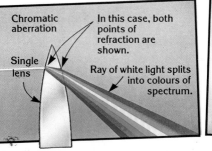

Chromatic aberration

In this case, both points of refraction are shown.

Single lens

Ray of white light splits into colours of spectrum.

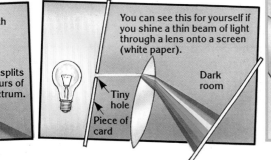

You can see this for yourself if you shine a thin beam of light through a lens onto a screen (white paper).

Dark room

Tiny hole

Piece of card

Looking after your microscope lenses

Dust and greasy marks on your microscope lenses will make the images you see much less sharp. Also, when you clean the lenses, the tiny dust particles will scratch their surfaces. Here are a few tips about looking after the lenses properly:

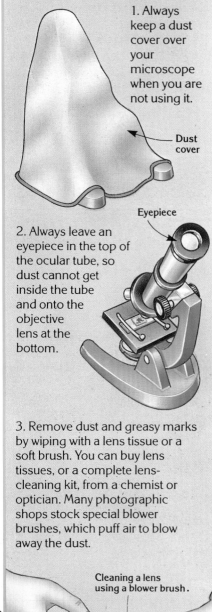

1. Always keep a dust cover over your microscope when you are not using it.

Dust cover

Eyepiece

2. Always leave an eyepiece in the top of the ocular tube, so dust cannot get inside the tube and onto the objective lens at the bottom.

3. Remove dust and greasy marks by wiping with a lens tissue or a soft brush. You can buy lens tissues, or a complete lens-cleaning kit, from a chemist or optician. Many photographic shops stock special blower brushes, which puff air to blow away the dust.

Cleaning a lens using a blower brush.

Objective lens

The electron microscope

Electron microscopes are large and complex. They use electrons instead of light, and magnify objects up to about 250 000 times, compared to about 2000 times for optical microscopes (see resolution and magnification on page 45). The images they produce are black and white, and are often given "false colour" (as shown on these two pages).

What are electrons?

Electrons are extremely tiny particles, thousands of times smaller than atoms. They have a negative electric charge and, because of the way magnetism works, this means their motion can be controlled by magnetic fields. In an electron microscope, magnets (called magnetic lenses) bend streams of electrons in the same way as glass lenses bend light rays in an optical microscope.

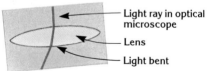

Light ray in optical microscope
Lens
Light bent

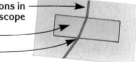

Beam of electrons in electron microscope
Magnetic field
Beam bent

The transmission electron microscope

The transmission electron microscope (TEM) works by "lighting up" a specimen on a stage with an electron stream, and focusing and magnifying the "image" with magnetic lenses. The electron image, which is invisible, is changed into a normal, visible image by using a special screen.

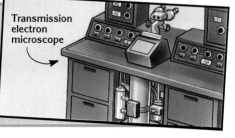

Transmission electron microscope

A fast-moving stream of electrons is produced by an electron gun at the top of the microscope. A very high electric voltage is needed to work the gun, so a special power supply is needed.

Inside the tube there is a vacuum (no air). This is because electrons are stopped by particles in air, so they would not get far in an air-filled tube.

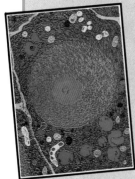

← False colour TEM photograph of a section of a cell in the root of a plant.

The electron stream is concentrated onto the specimen by a magnetic lens in the same way as a condenser focuses light (see page 8).

False colour TEM photograph of red blood cells moving through the walls of a blood vessel

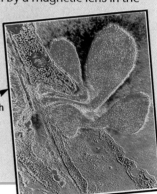

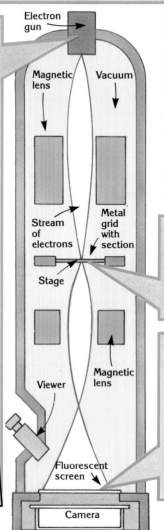

Electron gun

Magnetic lens

Vacuum

Stream of electrons

Metal grid with section

Stage

Magnetic lens

Viewer

Fluorescent screen

Camera

Specimens for electron microscopes need careful preparation. Living cells cannot be used, due to the vacuum – they would burst from the build-up of water pressure inside them. Specimens are often treated with chemicals to make features show up.

When cutting sections for the electron microscope, specimens are embedded in resin and cut using an ultramicrotome. The sections made are typically a hundred times thinner than those made for use in an optical microscope (see pages 24-25).

The electrons pass through the section (on a metal grid). Their paths are altered, making an image. This is focused and magnified by another magnetic lens.

Metal grid   Specimen

The electrons hit a fluorescent screen. The more electrons that hit each point, the brighter that point glows. This produces a visible image (recorded by a camera).

False colour TEM photograph of a section of a green alga (single-celled plant)

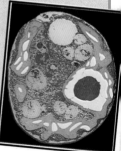

44

Resolution and magnification

The amount of detail which can be seen in an image is called its resolution. An optical microscope has a much greater resolving power than your eyes, so the images it produces have a higher resolution. The resolving power of the electron microscope is much greater still.

The eye can distinguish between objects which are down to 0.25mm apart before the objects blur together.

Light rays are is bent as they pass through an object, forming an image. Very small objects, though, do not affect light, so cannot be seen with an optical microscope. Once a certain magnification is reached, magnifying further will

Optical microscopes can distinguish objects 0.00025mm apart.

show up no more detail – the visible details just get bigger.

Electrons are affected by objects hundreds of times smaller than those which affect light. This means that an electron microscope has a much higher resolving power.

Electron microscopes can distinguish objects 0.0000005mm apart.

The scanning electron microscope

The scanning electron microscope (SEM) is used to examine the surface of objects. It produces images which are greatly magnified (up to 100 000 times) and show the actual shape of objects. As well as producing incredible pictures, the scanning electron microscope shows up detail which can be vitally important to scientists in many fields, such as medicine. It works by scanning the surface of an object with a thin electron beam.

False colour SEM photograph of the head of a black garden worker ant

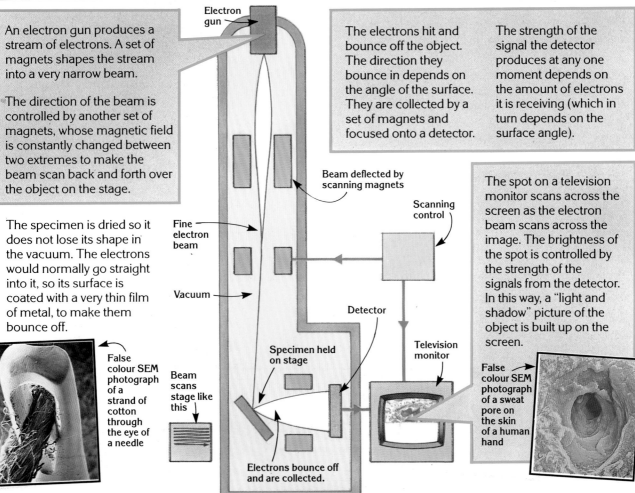

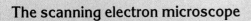

An electron gun produces a stream of electrons. A set of magnets shapes the stream into a very narrow beam.

The direction of the beam is controlled by another set of magnets, whose magnetic field is constantly changed between two extremes to make the beam scan back and forth over the object on the stage.

The specimen is dried so it does not lose its shape in the vacuum. The electrons would normally go straight into it, so its surface is coated with a very thin film of metal, to make them bounce off.

Electron gun

The electrons hit and bounce off the object. The direction they bounce in depends on the angle of the surface. They are collected by a set of magnets and focused onto a detector.

The strength of the signal the detector produces at any one moment depends on the amount of electrons it is receiving (which in turn depends on the surface angle).

Beam deflected by scanning magnets

Scanning control

The spot on a television monitor scans across the screen as the electron beam scans across the image. The brightness of the spot is controlled by the strength of the signals from the detector. In this way, a "light and shadow" picture of the object is built up on the screen.

Fine electron beam

Vacuum

False colour SEM photograph of a strand of cotton through the eye of a needle

Beam scans stage like this

Specimen held on stage

Detector

Television monitor

False colour SEM photograph of a sweat pore on the skin of a human hand

Electrons bounce off and are collected.

Equipment

Below is a basic list of equipment that you will find useful when working with your microscope. Some items can be obtained from hardware and chemist shops, and all of them should be available from specialist microscope shops, or scientific equipment suppliers.

The list does not include the individual things you need for the special projects in the book, such as making the jelly on page 16 or the hand microtome on page 24.

The pictures are not drawn to scale.

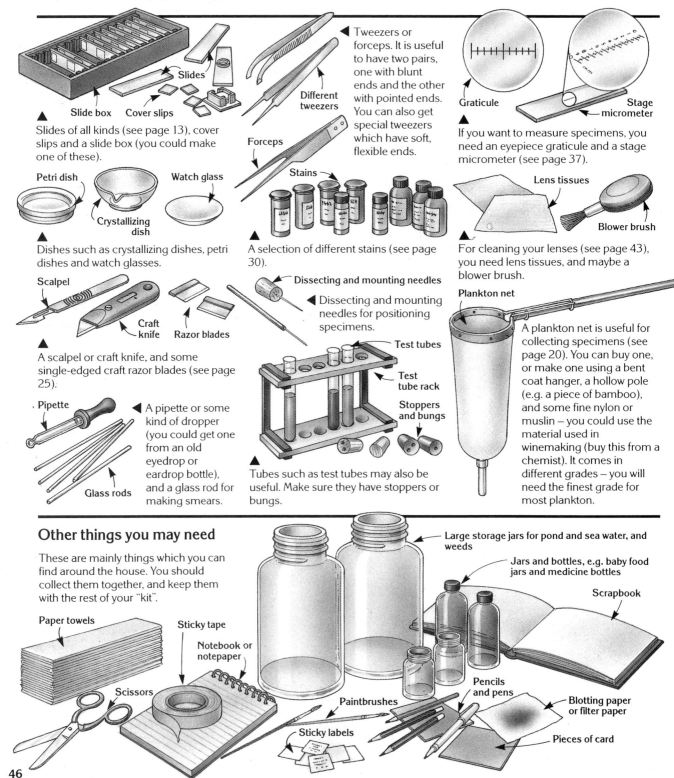

Slides of all kinds (see page 13), cover slips and a slide box (you could make one of these).

Slide box, Cover slips, Slides

Tweezers or forceps. It is useful to have two pairs, one with blunt ends and the other with pointed ends. You can also get special tweezers which have soft, flexible ends.

Different tweezers, Forceps

If you want to measure specimens, you need an eyepiece graticule and a stage micrometer (see page 37).

Graticule, Stage micrometer

Dishes such as crystallizing dishes, petri dishes and watch glasses.

Petri dish, Crystallizing dish, Watch glass

A selection of different stains (see page 30).

Stains

For cleaning your lenses (see page 43), you need lens tissues, and maybe a blower brush.

Lens tissues, Blower brush

A scalpel or craft knife, and some single-edged craft razor blades (see page 25).

Scalpel, Craft knife, Razor blades

Dissecting and mounting needles for positioning specimens.

Dissecting and mounting needles

A pipette or some kind of dropper (you could get one from an old eyedrop or eardrop bottle), and a glass rod for making smears.

Pipette, Glass rods

Tubes such as test tubes may also be useful. Make sure they have stoppers or bungs.

Test tubes, Test tube rack, Stoppers and bungs

A plankton net is useful for collecting specimens (see page 20). You can buy one, or make one using a bent coat hanger, a hollow pole (e.g. a piece of bamboo), and some fine nylon or muslin – you could use the material used in winemaking (buy this from a chemist). It comes in different grades – you will need the finest grade for most plankton.

Plankton net

Other things you may need

These are mainly things which you can find around the house. You should collect them together, and keep them with the rest of your "kit".

Paper towels, Sticky tape, Notebook or notepaper, Scissors, Paintbrushes, Sticky labels, Large storage jars for pond and sea water, and weeds, Jars and bottles, e.g. baby food jars and medicine bottles, Scrapbook, Pencils and pens, Blotting paper or filter paper, Pieces of card

Glossary

On this page, you will find a list of the more advanced terms which have been used in the book. The list also includes some other terms which you may come across in your further reading about the microscope.

Chromatic aberration. A common problem of single lenses. The different wavelengths of visible (white) light are refracted by slightly different amounts, as happens in a prism, and appear as a coloured halo (the colours of the spectrum) around the edges of the image.

Coarse adjustment/focusing knob. A focusing knob on an optical microscope for basic, coarse focusing. This is sufficient with low power lenses.

Dark ground illumination. A ▶ lighting technique for showing up detail in transparent objects. Only light which has reflected off the objects is allowed into the objective lens. This produces a view of bright objects on a dark background.

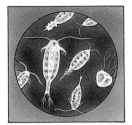

Decomposing. The breaking down of dead plant and animal matter, so that the basic chemicals of life they contain (mainly carbon and nitrogen) can be released back into nature's cycles. Decomposing is done by bacteria and fungi.

Depth of field/focus. The range over which an optical instrument will produce a focused image. A large depth of focus, such as that of a stereoscopic microscope, means that manual focusing is easier and only needs coarse adjustment, rather than fine adjustment.

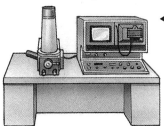

◀ **Electron microscope.** A microscope which uses beams of electrons (subatomic particles) to produce images, instead of using light, as optical microscopes do. There are a number of different types.

Field of view. The whole area visible under a microscope.

Fine adjustment/focusing knob. A focusing knob on a microscope for very fine focusing adjustments, such as those needed with high power lenses.

Fixative. A preservative whose preserving powers last even after it has been washed away. It actually changes the structure of the tissue it is added to.

Graticule. Any regular pattern of lines ▶ which can be reproduced on a marked scale to give a measurement. An eyepiece graticule is a graticule on clear film or glass which fits into the eyepiece of a microscope.

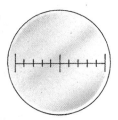

Inverted microscope. A microscope, often binocular or stereoscopic, where the stage is at the top, and the viewing system is underneath. Prisms are used to refract the light round the ocular tube, which is normally angled in two places, so that you look downwards, as usual, but see upwards.

Magnification. The degree of enlargement of an image produced by an optical instrument.

Magnifying power. The capability of an optical instrument to produce different levels of magnification.

Micrometer. Any instrument used to measure tiny distances. A stage micrometer is a micrometer consisting of a scale etched on clear film or a glass slide. It is placed on the stage of a microscope, like any other slide.

Non-vital staining. The staining of dead plant or animal tissue.

Photomicrograph. A photograph taken of an image made by an optical or an electron microscope.

Polarizing microscope. A ▶ microscope which incorporates pieces of polarizing material. These produce polarized light (light in one plane only) from normal light. Polarizing microscopes are mainly used for viewing mineral crystals and metals.

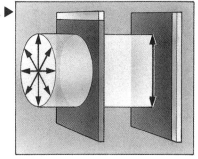

Preferential staining. The process in which certain stains "prefer" some substances in a specimen to others. Hence they stain some, but not all, of the features in the specimen.

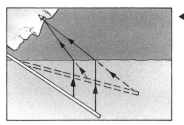

◀ **Refraction.** The "bending" of a wave (e.g. a light wave) when it moves from one medium into another, which causes it to move at a different velocity (e.g. from air into glass).

Resolution. The degree of detail of a visible object or the image of that object.

Resolving power. The capability of the eye or an optical instrument to produce different levels of resolution.

Vital staining. The staining of live plant or animal tissue.

Index

Accessories (microscope) 9
Algae, 21, 22
Antonie van Leeuwenhoek, 4
Aperture control, 8, 11
Archaeology (microscope uses), 40-41
Atoms, 5

Bacteria, 4, 16-17
Binocular microscope, 4
Blood, 5, 31
Bottom lighting, 10
Bread mould, 19

Cells, 4, 5, 14-15, 25, 26-27, 30-31
Chloroplasts, 15
Chromatic aberration, 43, 47
Coarse adjustment (focusing) knob, 47
Colour filters, 31
Compound eyes, 29
Compound lens, 43
Condenser (condensing lens), 8
Crystals, 34-35
Cytoplasm, 15

Dark ground illumination, 20, 47
Decomposing, 16, 18, 47
Depth of field (focus), 47
Dust, 13

Electron(s), 44
Electronics (microscope uses), 40
Electron microscope, 4, 5, 44-45, 47
- scanning, 45
- transmission, 44
Environment (testing), 41
Equipment, 46
Etching, 33
Eyepiece (eye lens), 8
- graticule, 37, 46, 47

Fabrics, 7
Feathers, 12
Fibres, 7, 38, 39, 41
Field lens, 6
Field microscope, 9
Field of view, 47
Fine adjustment (focusing) knob, 47
Fingerprints, 38, 39
Fingertip test for bacteria, @16
Fixative, 36, 37, 47
Flowers, 27
Focusing, 8, 11, 47
Food,
- development, 41
- preservation, 41
- testing for bacteria, 17
Forensic science (microscope uses), 38
Freshwater,
- plant and animal life, 22-23
Fungi, 18-19
- spores, 19, 41

Geology (microscope uses), 32-33, 35, 38
Glass, 12, 42

Graticule, 46, 47
- eyepiece, 37, 47

Hairs, 12
History (microscope), 4-5

Illumination system, 8
Images, 42-43
Industry (microscope uses), 40
Insects, 28
- slide trap, 3, 28
Inverted microscope, 47

Leaves, 27
Lens(es), 4, 42-43
- cleaning, 43
- compound, 43
- eye(piece), 8
- field, 6
- objective, 8, 10
- water-drop, 4
Lighting,
- bottom (transmitted), 10
- top, 13
Linen tester, see Piece glass

Magnetic lenses, 44
Magnification, 9, 45, 47
Magnifying box, 6
Magnifying glasses, 6-7, 42
Magnifying power, 9, 47
Materials research (microscope uses), 40
Measuring specimens, 36-37
Medicine (microscope uses), 38
Metals, 40
Microfossils, 33, 38
Micrometer, 46, 47
- stage, 37, 47
Microscopic scale, 5
Microtomes, 24-25, 37
Minerals, 32-33, 35
Mounting, 14-15, 36-37
Multi-ocular microscope, 4, 9

Non-vital staining, 47
Nosepiece, 8, 10

Objective lens(es), 8, 10
Ocular tube, 10
Oil exploration, 33, 38
Optical microscope,
- parts of, 8

Paper fibres, 7
Permanent mounting, 36-37
Photomicrograph, 47
Piece glass, 6
Plankton, 20
Plant sections, 25, 26-27, 30-31
Polarized light, 35
Polarizing microscope, 35, 47
Polishing rocks, 33

Pollen, 27, 40, 41
Pollution, 41
Preferential staining, 30, 47
Printing, 6
Projector screen, 9

Quality control, 40

Refraction, 42, 43, 47
Resolution, 45, 47
Resolving power, 45, 47
Robert Hooke, 4, 15
Rock(s), 32-33, 35
Rock pools,
- plant and animal life, 21
Roots and root hairs, 26

Scale, 5
Sea,
- plant and animal life, 20-21
Sectioning and sections, 24-27, 36, 37
Semi-permanent mounting, 36
Skin, 7
Slides, 11, 13, 46
Smears, 14, 31
Soil, 35
- animal life, 23
Soot, 13, 41
Stage, 8, 11
- micrometer, 37, 46, 47
Staining and stains, 30-31
Stems, 26
Stereo magnifier, 7
- headband, 6
Stereomicroscope, 9

Telescope, 5
Temporary mounting, 14-15, 36
Tissue specimens, 25, 36, 37
Top lighting, 13
Transmitted lighting, see Bottom lighting
Tripod magnifying glass, 6

Vacuoles, 15, 30, 31
Vegetables, 27, 30
Viruses, 17, 38
Vital staining, 47

Watchmaker's eyeglass, 6
Water-drop lens, 4
Wood, 27

Yeast, 18, 19
Zoom eyepiece, 8

The photographs on pages 44 and 45 were
kindly supplied by the Science Photo Library,
Westbourne Grove, London.